BURY

The Golden Years

1900s to 1970s

The publishers would like to thank the following companies for their support in the production of this book

Albany International

Dunsters Farm

Hargreaves Ductwork Ltd

Holy Cross College

Jetchem Systems Ltd

Milliken Industrials Ltd

Wallwork Heat Treatment Ltd

William Hare Group

First published in Great Britain by True North Books Limited

England HX3 6SN

01422 244555

www.truenorthbooks.com

INTRODUCTION

For all of us, memories are the currency which we use to record the changes and progress in our everyday lives and to fix our place as individuals in the greater scheme of things. The is the latest publication in our 'Memories' series of publications, covering nostalgic reflections of towns and cities throughout the UK. In this new book we will be meandering through a pictorial cross-section of life in Bury over the last 100 years or so, to help satisfy the longing we all get from time to time, to recall memories of a different era that now seems better or simpler.

As we get older it is often easier to take a step back, and to view events and developments with a clearer sense of prospective. Our aim has been to assist in this respect by presenting a publication relevant to the area capable of rekindling memories of days gone by in an entertaining and informative manner. Looking through the pages of this book it is interesting to reflect on exactly how much change has taken place in the area over a short period, relative to its long history. Many of these photographs are unique and will inevitably remind us of experiences and events in our lives, of our families and of those whose influence and support has touched us to a greater or lesser degree.

Defining features about nostalgia are universal and can bring back fond memories from a time gone by. Recent research shows that nostalgia can counteract loneliness, boredom and anxiety. Couples feel closer and look happier when they're sharing nostalgic memories. People generally get a 'Warm Glow' inside when relating to events and occasions in the past and enjoy reminiscences about how things used to be - even when these events sometimes have a painful side. When people speak wistfully of the past, they typically become more optimistic and inspired about the future.

We can all remember events surrounding friends and family, holidays, weddings, special occasions and nights out in Bury. So let your mind wander and think of the youthful days at the dance hall or courting in one of the many cinemas in the city. Be entertained as we take you on a sentimental journey through the pages of Bury - The Golden Years... Happy Memories!

TEXT	ANDREW MITCHELL, BRENDAN O'NEILL
COMPANY PROFILES	STEPHEN FIRTH
PHOTOGRAPHS	BRENDAN O'NEILL
DESIGNER	CHRIS THORPE
BUSINESS DEVELOPMENT MANAGER	PETER PREST

CONTENTS

VIEWS OF VICTORIAN & EDWARDIAN BURY

The Derby Hotel, on the right, joined with the Athenaeum and the Derby Hall to form an integrated complex all the way down to Kay Gardens. Situated in Market Place, the hotel opened its doors in 1850. The Earl of Derby was the driving force behind the building work and had commissioned the notable architect Sidney Smirke to undertake the main design. Included in the fabric was stabling for 15 horses, a reflection on the main form of road transport used in Victorian times. The delightfully appointed hotel played host to royalty and other distinguished guests over the years. However, nothing lasts forever and time was called in the early 1960s when the brewery decided its course was run. The Derby Hotel was demolished in 1965, leaving the parish church of St Mary the Virgin to continue to fly the flag for buildings of architectural interest on The Rock.

Above: Kay Gardens were laid out from 1903 in honour of the man who made a major contribution to the production of woven cloth. They were officially opened in 1908 by the wife of the donor, Henry Whitehead, who also provided the domed memorial created by sculptor W Venn Gough, a native of Bristol. Lord Derby unveiled the 35 foot Portland stone structure later that same day. It was erected on a sandstone base rescued from the old market building that stood here from 1839 until it was demolished in 1901, when the new market was opened. John Kay (1704-79) is one of the names in the history of textile production that locals fondly recall. He invented the flying shuttle, a piece of equipment that helped a weaver work on wider fabrics in an industry that became more mechanised as time went by.

Right: The tramlines on Market Street, together with the overhead power cabling, place this image in the late Edwardian era. Modern day youngsters regard trams as a phenomenon born in the latter years of the 20th century, having grown up with Metrolink on their doorsteps. They are more than a little surprised to learn that we had a service as far back as 1883, when horses were the power source. Electrification by the Bury Corporation Tramway Company took place in 1903 and trams continued to be in service until 1949, though their use had been reduced during the 1930s. The elegant Victorian building on the right was built in 1860 to house the Manchester and District Banking Company. The entrance doorway is flanked by Tuscan columns. In more recent times it has been home of a Yates Winebar.

Frederick W Purcell was a Victorian theatre proprietor well known in the north-west, running successful enterprises in Derby and Rochdale. He opened the Theatre Royal and Opera House on Market Street in 1899. The entertainment centre dominated the locality for the best part of the next century before being replaced by various retail outlets. Designed by Frank Matcham, it was a handsome building with its impressive façade. The interior was similarly imposing, having three balconies supported by six fine pillars. The theatre was converted into a full time cinema in 1933, with art deco alterations to the interior and rebranding as the Royal Cinema. Further changes took place in the 1970s when it became known as the Essoldo and, later, the Classic. Those of us who had done our courting on the back row, now only have memories to cling to as it was demolished in 1985.

It was in 1440 that King Henry VI acknowledged Bury's growth in importance by granting the town the right to hold a market. Surrounded by alehouses, of which the Two Tubs is the sole survivor, this was the equivalent of a shopping centre in the 18th century. The Market Hall and change seem to go hand in hand when discussing the history of this site and it gets confusing when talking of the old and new buildings as the descriptions refer to different ones, depending upon when the discussion takes place! By the start of the Victorian era, the market place had become inadequate and dangerous,

with stalls so close to each other that they obstructed the general flow of shoppers. A new market was established in 1837 on land that was later to be used as Kay Gardens. In 1901, with the Market Hall being regarded as insecure, the pictured building was introduced as a replacement. It served us well until gutted by a devastating fire in November 1968. A temporary hall was set up until the next one was established on its present site in 1971. Further construction was completed by the end of the last century.

Right: In the days before the First World War things continued as much they had in Edwardian times. The horse still provided some of the muscle for transporting both goods and people, but change was in the air. Motorised private vehicles and public transport powered by electricity had started to alter how some of us got into town from the outlying districts. Policemen, such as this one on Silver Street, were deployed to help control traffic, their job descriptions now including chasing errant drivers as well as thieves and vagabonds.

Above: The Boer War Memorial was erected in Market Square in 1905. Situated in Market Place, across the way from the Parish Church, it showed a Lancashire Fusilier lifting his busby in honour of his monarch, whilst honouring the loss of comrades on foreign fields. It was unveiled by the 17th Earl of Derby, but was moved in 1920 when a large tram shelter was erected on the original site. It now stands in front of the Town Hall in Whitehead Tower Gardens.

Right: This is a rare early photograph of children playing outside Emanuel Holcombe School in 1906. The Church of England Primary School lies on the main road just north of the centre of Holcombe village. It was built about 1870, shortly after Emmanuel church, and has always had links with it. The school's position alongside a relatively unobstructed Helmshore Road was clearly not an issue in an era when motorised transport was not a factor in day to day life, as it would be today. The building was damaged by a bomb in the Zeppelin raid in 1916 and the only known casualty, a thrush, is preserved in a glass case in the school. The girls are wearing the white over-pinafores, which presumably washed more easily than the dresses underneath. The boys look smart too, some in breeches and 'sailor tops'.

Above: Openshaw is not only a district of Manchester, but also the surname of prominent cotton manufacturers who were busy locally during the period of our history we now refer to as the Industrial Revolution. The Jubilee Fountain on Manchester Road, pictured a century ago, was donated by Eliza, daughter of Oliver Ormerod Openshaw, to mark the 60th anniversary of the date on which Queen Victoria came to the throne. Designed by Thomas Rogers Kitsell, it was sited at the junction with Manchester Old Road in 1897. Granted listed status in 1985, it is still there today.

Left and right: Photographs from late Victorian times, in the latter years of the 19th century, show just how gloomy and dingy the living conditions were for many households. The whitewash on the walls in Back Fleet Street (right) does not hide the obvious signs of damp that are evident at ground level. This type of housing, close to the area later known as The Rock, was where the working classes had to live a hand to mouth existence, while the mill owners and other members of the middle class enjoyed homes with running water, proper sanitary facilities and servants to carry out mundane tasks on their behalf. The rare but rather grainy photograph on the left shows residents posing in the yard at Albert Court, off Bolton Road, who also had to endure cramped premises. Little wonder that average life expectancy back then was just 45 years.

Above: This is a brilliantly nostalgic image of three generations of one family, standing on the pavement outside their back to back home. This would be the family home for the next two generations. Back-to- back housing was a pragmatic approach to the acute housing shortage of the latter half of the 19th century. The ever increasing population of the North's industrial towns and cities led to more and more folk being crammed into smaller and smaller spaces. Tens of thousands of speculative, often jerrybuilt, back-to-back houses were constructed. On hilly sites the back-to-back element was also part of an up-and-over building scheme, with 'under dwellings a common feature as well as landing-access only. Most were demolished in slum clearances in the 1960s.

BUILDINGS & MONUMENTS

Above: Looking along Walmersley Road up towards Limefield Brow, for over a century this site has been home to a quaintly named pub. Originally this was The Hark to Towler Inn, a reference to a warning given to people that the taxman was approaching. 'Towler' is derived from 'tolier' or 'toller', spellings used in medieval times to refer to the holder of that dreaded occupation. The pub now just uses the job title as its name and you might think that the word is unique in its use in the licensing trade, but you would be mistaken. Although unusual, it appears on a number of local watering holes, such as The Hark to Towler on Bury New Road, Heywood and The Towler in Market Street, Tottington.

Right: Being a vicar or parish priest is very much a 24 hour job, as the vicarage or presbytery is usually alongside the central place of worship. The rectory associated with the parish church of St Mary the Virgin is no different from others in this respect. The word used to refer to the home of a minister of a church can vary, often dependent upon the rank of the occupant or his denomination. A bishop lives in a palace and a dean in a deanery, but a Scottish cleric might reside in a manse and a Lutheran in a parsonage. When referring to their homes, Anglicans generally use rectory or vicarage, as to whichever takes the fancy.

Above: The Castle Armoury is the largest Army Reserve Centre in Britain. Its Drill Hall echoed to the sound of marching boots when this record of the building was captured. In more recent times it has been used to host large wedding receptions, boxing tournaments, concerts, antique fairs and exhibitions. It was built in 1868 to house the 8th Lancashire Rifle Volunteers on the site of Bury Castle, re-using some of the old building materials. It was extended in 1907 in the same loosely medieval style to provide the drill hall we see here.

Above: On any day of the week you would expect the entrance area of a hospital to be a place of high activity. This was not the case when this pre First World War image was captured as the scene was surprisingly quiet. Here we see the lodge of the old infirmary on the corner of Walmersley Road and Mosley Avenue. The former building still stands, but the site where the Dispensary Hospital could once be found is now home to a collection of apartment blocks. Founded in 1882, it became known as the Infirmary in 1928.

Above: Was this young chap one of the lucky ones to be in receipt of a 'proper education'? He is well turned out and seems to be clutching a set of books and papers that could have been part of homework or projects set for him by his form master. Life at school in the Edwardian era was very different to how it is now. Children were in fact quite lucky, as they were at school and not working. A generation earlier, in the 1860s, one third of children in England did not attend school at all and right up until 1881 children were not required to go. Only in the 20th century were young children no longer regularly expected to work alongside adults. By 1918 school attendance was not only compulsory but the school leaving age was raised from 12 to 14 years old. Edwardian schools were similar in a lot of ways to modern ones. Classes were taken in the 'three R's' (reading, writing and arithmetic) and there were also physical education lessons.

The Whitehead Clock Tower is a prominent feature in each of the accompanying photographs and is one of Bury's most attractive landmarks. Built of Portland stone on a stepped plinth of Aberdeen granite, it has looked out across its accompanying gardens since before the Great War of 1914-18. Built on the site of a former private lunatic asylum, it owes its existence to the determination of Henry Whitehead to erect a memorial to his brother, Walter, a prominent surgeon who died in 1913. Less than 12 months after his death, the tower and surrounding gardens were declared open by a fellow medical man, Sir Frederick Treves, the doctor who befriended Joseph Merrick, the 'Elephant Man'. Henry Whitehead was also the inspiration behind the provision of the Kay Memorial in the town centre. In the Manchester Road image, below, the Town Hall is clearly seen in the background. This seat of local government opened in 1954. The town council should have moved from its former place on Market Street and made the nearby Derby Hall its base, but a spat with Lord Derby meant that the elected members refused to meet there, though it was used by a magistrates' court and petty session. The Boer War Memorial with its soldier on the plinth was moved here in 1920.

Standing in front Robert Peel's statue is the memorial to those who gave their lives for our country out in South Africa during the 1900-02 Boer War. Seen in its original place on Market Square, it was dedicated in particular to the 170 men who lost their lives in service with the Lancashire Fusiliers. The 2nd Battalion was heavily involved at Spion Kop and in the Relief of Ladysmith. The regiment had been formed in 1881 when several other battalions and militia were amalgamated. In 1898, the Fusiliers took part in Kitchener's campaign in the Sudan, taking a prominent role in the Battle of Omdurman. Some eighteen of its men and officers were awarded the Victoria Cross during the First World War.

Above: This fine house in Holcombe Brook was the former home of the Aitken family, built in 1846 of stone and slate in a gabled and decorative style popular with Victorians. Known then as Lower Hey House, it was extended in 1864 and after the family had left, turned into a sanatorium and TB isolation hospital. The verandas that were added offered patients the chance to sit out in the fresh air that doctors hoped would help their recovery. That might have been a pious hope, considering what was belching out from factory chimneys not far away. After it closed, the building became derelict in the early 1970s, but was then taken over by Darul Uloom, as an Islamic educational centre for boys and young men.

Right: The Albion Hotel on Haymarket Street is another of those town centre pubs now firmly placed in the memory banks of more elderly drinkers who once supped here. It belonged to the Bury Brewery Company that stood on George Street, another of those independents that could not stay in business when faced by strong competition from the 'big boys'. It also seems that the days are gone when public bars echoed to the click of dominoes or the tapping of matchsticks on a crib board.

Below: To the left of the Parish Church, Sir Robert Peel still stands on his plinth today. The vista around The Rock has changed considerably and now lacks the gentle, calm atmosphere those sitting quietly on benches across the road could enjoy in c1960. At least our famous son remains in place, as does the war memorial that was unveiled in 1924 to honour those killed in the Great War. Sadly, more names were added after World War II. St Mary's Church has a history dating back to before the Domesday Book was compiled. It was rebuilt in the 13th century and restored in 1535. Further reconstructed in the 18th century, the present incarnation dates from the 1870s.

Above: This photograph from the late 1950s, looks like it was taken on a Sunday as it is unusual for the Market Place to be so quiet. A lone Ford Consul II is parked outside Eric Suddell's Opticians. Some older readers may well remember the distinguishing features of this car, with a bench front seat

trimmed in PVC, and the handbrake was operated by an umbrella-style pull lever under the dash. The opticians, along with the former Lloyds Bank building, built around 1870, on the corner of Bolton Street, have now become a pub and bar. Much of this area around the Robert Peel statue, on the right, is now paved. The Peel Memorial commemorates the life of Sir Robert Peel, twice UK Prime Minister and founder of the British Conservative Party, who was born in Bury. The statue is by Edward Hodges Baily, a nineteenth-century British artist best known for his sculpture of Nelson on Nelson's Column.

SURROUNDING AREAS

Holly Mount at Tottington offered a delightful, rural view in 1910. The village lies between Bury and Ramsbottom on the edge of the West Pennine Moors and the Rossendale Valley. The Peel Monument can be glimpsed on the distant hillside from many spots in and around the vicinity. The memorial tower to Sir Robert Peel, also known as "Holcombe Tower", high above Ramsbottom was planned and erected at the same time as Bury was preparing its statue to the then recently deceased statesman who was born in Bury. It was opened in 1852 in memory of Robert Peel, the famous son of Bury who twice served the nation as its Prime Minister. Tottington is the birthplace of two 'Coronation Street' actors in Antony Cotton (born Dunn), who plays the role of Sean Tully, and Vicky Binns, who played Molly Dobbs, a character killed off in 2010. Lisa Riley, the TV presenter and actress, is also a native of this village. Wallace and Gromit fans will also point out that a certain Lady Tottington was Wallace's love interest in 'The Curse of the Were-Rabbit'!

Left: This image is of the village centre in c1900. Female fashion was all long skirts, while menfolk usually wore jackets and shirts with collars and ties. People felt undressed if they wore anything else. Tottington's name is most likely derived from the Old English for the land or farmstead belonging to a man called Tota; or "tot" may be from an Old English word meaning "hilltop lookout point". Since the Second World War Tottington has expanded with the Moorside Area residential development being built in the early 1970s and new property built on the site of many of the former mills such as Spring Mill and Kirklees Mill.

Right and below: Chapel Street leads down the hill from Market Street, taking us towards Tottington and the Parish Church of St Anne. This centre of worship has been here since 1799, owing its origins to the benevolence of John Gorton, a businessman who made his fortune in the cotton trade. He was also responsible for funding the refurbishment of Tottington Hall. The church has seen many changes over time, but was nearly lost to the village when German V-1 rockets blew out most of its windows in a raid during the last war. Happily, it survived and continues to serve its congregation into another century. The houses on the left have gone now and replaced by a beautiful green space, with trees and park style benches.

Right: Brookhouse in Tottington has, in more recent times, been separated into two housing units as 131 and 133 Holcombe Road. Woodland to the west and access to Old Kay's Park close by help this area keep its semi rural feel, despite the busy road that lost its cobblestones many years ago. The bridge was widened as traffic demands increased and some of the cottages pictured were demolished. The children in the distance were standing at the start of the incline known as Stormer Hill. The way to Greenmount is behind the photographer. The large garden opposite Brookhouse was tended by the Lomax family in the early 1900s.

Below: It is hard to imagine a more nostalgic view of Balderstone from the beginning of the last century. The photographer, from his elevated position, has managed to capture a herd cows along the road, a horse and cart, the church spire, a multi-wired telegraph pole and an ornate gas street light. Not to mention the group of women wearing clogs and shawls, who had got together for a good old chinwag. Grouped on the corner of the street, they were possibly discussing the latest excesses of the Prince of Wales, the future Edward VII who was seldom out of the limelight thanks to his interest in pleasure first and public duty second.

Above and below: The similar pair of views across to Holcombe Hill were taken from Longsight and the slope at Brookhouse, respectively. In both pictures we can make out the outline of the structure known to some as Holcombe Tower. This is the memorial to Robert Peel, the politician born in Ramsbottom who went on to achieve fame in Westminster, initially as the Home Secretary who helped pioneer the reform of criminal law and play a lead role in establishing the modern police service. A walk up the hill on a summer evening is well rewarded by the vista from the top across the moors and on into Manchester, Cheshire and even North Wales on a clear day. The return journey down into the village can be finished off with a pint or two in the lounge bar of the Shoulder of Mutton.

Hollins Lane in Unsworth is now much leafier than it appeared over a century ago. It is also a much busier road, serving one of the Bury suburbs that lies close to the townís main golf course. The little girls pictured on the left would not have much interest in the niblicks, mashies or spoons that golfers used to hit balls back then. They

played with their own simple toys, using skipping ropes, a top and a whip or just a simple bat and ball. If we were to think sexist thoughts it might be suggested that our featured trio was obviously practising for womanhood, as the girls were chattering away non-stop. Although some might think that, we could not possibly comment!

Even small villages had their own railway station in the days long before Mr Beeching produced the mid 1960s report that heralded the closure of many of our local lines. Remarkably, he was rewarded with a peerage for providing the ammunition that fired up one the most unpopular pieces of transport legislation of the 20th century. Beeching was just a twinkle in his parents' eye when Greenmount Station was photographed. However, the man who was nicknamed 'Butcher Beeching' could not be blamed for the loss of this service as it was withdrawn in 1952. This local line was opened by the Bury and Tottington Railway Company in 1882, offering a connection with Holcombe Brook. The image dates from the first decade of the last century.

The name Affetside means 'boundary on the hill, which is appropriate as this village is some 900 feet above sea level. It is situated on the line of the old Roman road known as Watling Street that ran from Manchester to Ribchester. Affetside took on some small significance in the 18th century, thanks to its position on a packhorse route. The name of the village's Pack Horse Inn is a lasting testament to that era, though there has been a hostelry on this site since the 15th century. The history of the cross on the edge of the village green is the subject of some discussion. Some believe it to be Roman in origin, while others feel it is more likely to have been a medieval marker for pilgrims en route to Whalley Abbey.

ENTERTAINMENT & EVENTS

Patriotic pride in the royal family and a chance to get a glimpse of them in the flesh, brought out huge crowds of Bury folk, as we can see in this photograph from July, 1921. The occasion was the visit of Prince Edward, the Prince of Wales, on a tour of Lancashire towns. Onlookers lined the streets and waved flags as the royal procession went by. As the motorcade swept the future King Edward VIII into town, along Market Street, people cheered and threw their hats in

the air. The heir to the throne was taking lunch with Lord Derby and other dignitaries at Derby Hall, seen on the left of this picture. The building designed by Sidney Smirke was opened in 1850. This complex also included the elegant facade of the Derby Hotel and Athenaeum, which was a much loved landmark for many years in Bury. The difficult times meant a limited amount of banners and decorations, as highlighted outside the Tea & Coffeee Rooms opposite.

Bury FC is one of the country's longest serving members of the Football League. Founded in 1885, the club has played at Gigg Lane throughout its history. The smartly attired XI, in handsome striped shirts and dickie bows, is the team that won the 1892 Lancashire Challenge Cup. Two years later, Bury was elected to the Football League and won the Second Division title that very first season. More success followed in the next decade when our side won the FA Cup in 1900 and again in 1903, the latter victory being a 6-0 score that has never been bettered in a final. The 1908 side in the picture included Billy Hibbert, one of only five Bury players to have represented England.

Soccer has its Billy Meredith and cricket its WG Grace, but to golfers it is the name of Harry Vardon that conjures up images of sporting greatness from the turn into the last century. Born in Jersey in 1870, he showed a natural aptitude for the game from a young age, but his playing opportunities were limited as his parents lacked the financial means to support him. So, Harry moved to England as a greenkeeper at Studley Royal Golf Club in Ripon, before becoming the professional at Bury in 1891, the club having only just opened in the previous year. Vardon spent five years with us before acquiring superstar status in 1896 when he won the Open Championship at Muirfield. In all, he would top this leader board on six occasions, a record that has still not been beaten. His then unusual method of gripping a club, using interlocking fingers, is still the most popular one adopted today.

Union Square was once the vibrant hub of the town, as we can see in this picture from 1939. Thousands of Bury folk had turned out for the traditional Whit Walk and they had all gathered in the 'Square'. Historians have traced the first 'walks' back to around 1800, arising out of the Sunday School movement which began in 1784. Whitsuntide later became an annual holiday when workers took advantage of the mills closing down for the day. During the 19th century Whitsuntide became an accepted holiday week for all, with the mills shutting down and the workers taking canal boat trips

and later, with the coming of the railways, cheap rail excursions. The original Union Square, which can be seen in this photograph, was knocked down in the 1960s to make way for what ultimately became part of the Mill Gate shopping centre. As a direct result the name was lost, but now the name of Union Square has been resurrected, and is the name for the new public square at Knowsley Place.

Above: A rag and bone man (far right) makes his way along Silver Street passed the heavily decorated Bury municipal offices and council chamber. He may well be oblivious to the forthcoming jubilee events linked to the 50th anniversary of Bury achieving borough status. Flags and bunting festooned the whole of Bury so they would have been hard to miss. On the corner of Bank Street, the impressive stone building was built in 1836 and is now Grade II listed. It was built for Bury Banking Company who amalgamated with the Lancashire and Yorkshire Bank in 1888. More recently it was home to Barclays Bank and is close to many of the town's long established professional businesses and adjacent to both the Lancashire Fusilier Museum and Library.

Right: It was possibly not the best vantage point for this photographer to capture the Radcliffe Children's procession in the 1950s as the concrete lamp post seems to obscure a good deal of the shot. However, a cold day and a little light drizzle wouldn't dampen the sprits of these group of well turned out youngsters who would have been looking forward to their May procession. With mums, dads, aunts and uncles all watching proudly in their gabardines, flat caps and warm woollen coats, it was a day to celebrate for the people of Bury.

Above: In this image we can see a procession of female Whit Walkers from 1953, on the cobbled streets in Bury. The ladies from St Joseph's Church are all dressed in their Sunday best for the walk through town. It was a hot sunny day but most of the female participants still had on their hat and coat. It was an important social event in the calendar and many of these ladies would have saved up especially to buy a new frock for the occasion. The Whit Walk was abandoned in the mid 1960s when Spring Bank Holiday replaced the Friday as a public holiday.

Right: We can see from this 1930 photograph that the Whit Walk procession went ahead despite the horrible weather conditions. The Bury crowds had still come out in force to line the streets as the parade passed through the town. Here we can four young boys and girls dressed in national costume, walking on the slippery cobbles along The Rock. It is not clear why they should choose to wear South American costumes for the event. They were carrying on a tradition that historians have traced back to around 1800, arising out of a Sunday School movement which aimed to ensure child mill workers steered clear of vices such as drinking and gambling. However it then became seen as a 'procession of witness' and a public declaration of faith. As an annual event, it reached its peak in the 1920s and 1930s.

Cycling can attract large crowds, as seen in the main photograph during the race on the track at Pilot Mill, on Alfred Road during the last war. In modern times it has become big news in the sports bulletins. Names such as Chris Hoy, Mark Cavendish, Victoria Pendleton, Laura Trott and Bradley Wiggins are just a handful of those who feature regularly on the back pages, as they whizz around the track or out on the open road. So popular is the sport these days that the three men mentioned have all won the BBC Sports Personality of the Year Award, in 2008, 2011 and 2012 respectively. Beforehand, only Tommy Simpson in 1965 achieved that accolade. But, if the trophy had been around in the 1940s then Reg Harris would surely have been on the podium. Born in Birtle in 1920, he joined the Bury section of the Cyclists' Touring Club, winning his first open age competitive race as a mere 15 year old. He had just achieved international selection when war broke out. He was wounded on active service, but returned to full fitness in peacetime and won the world amateur sprint title in 1947. The image of above, Reg leading Dennis Talbot round the track was taken at Herne Hill that same year. The individual picture shows him riding in the 1948 Olympic Games, when he won two silver medals. He had been expected to win golds, but was handicapped by broken ribs and a damaged elbow sustained in accidents not long before the tournament opened. Harris turned professional after the Olympics and won the world professional sprint title on four occasions, becoming a household name in the process.

Taking place only a few miles out of Bury was the 1956 Prestwich Carnival, which had as usual attracted a large number of people to the annual event. The Prestwich carnival has its roots in various traditions that stretch back into the mists of time. The very smartly dressed girls in the foreground would probably have been part of a parade or demonstration taking place on the day. As a special treat, the girls would have tucked into potted meat paste sandwiches washed down with Vimto. Then there was the appeal of the cake stands, craft stalls and games of skill to play. Back in the middle of the 19th century, Prestwich Wakes entertainment would have included events like, 'A foot race for a Beaver hat', 'A sack race', A sticky 'eating match of 3lb of treacle & bread' and possibly 'Porridge eating'. To the right of the image, one of the Morris Men, in traditional costume, had slipped away from his colleagues and was making his way through the crowds. The Morris Men bands were a sight to be seen and as well as entertaining the crowd, also provided a link with some of the pagan rituals of days gone by.

Right: There was just time to get a quick group photograph before these predominently female workforce board the 'Charra' to go on a day trip to the seaside. Just over thirty members of staff from Ringmill's are about to set off on a great adventure. The year was 1947 so they would have had very little to get excited about in interim, since the end of WWII. The ladies understandably look to be well wrapped up to cope with the elements that they might encounter on the outing. The 1940s and 50s were relatively hard times due to national recovery being slow after the War; rationing was still evident and annual holidays had not really become established for poorer workers such as weavers and spinners, so a day's outing to the seaside was a rare treat and all that some workers with large families could afford. "Charabanc trips" were usually only for adults, again due to finance. Occasionally the mill owner would help to pay for these outings, but this was not always the case.

Above: The Theatre Royal and Opera House opened on 26, December, 1889 and became one of the most popular theatres in the north of England. Designed by Frank Matcham, the building was to dominate the entertainment scene in Bury for the next 96 years. It was situated in the centre of the town, opposite the famous Market Hall at the corner of Market Street and Princess Street. Some of the biggest names performed here, including Sir Henry Irvine, Fred Karno's Circus and the great, Charlie Chaplin. By 1914 it had been taken over by Halifax based Northern Theatres Co. Inc. From 1933 it became a full time cinema. At the time of this photograph in 1954, the film showing was The Runaway Bus, a British comedy film starring Frankie Howerd, Margaret Rutherford and Petula Clark. In 1971 the circle area was sealed off and the extended stalls cinema was renamed Essoldo, but the following year saw another round of alterations as the cinema was taken over by the London based Classic Cinemas chain. It closed on 9 May, 1985 and was swiftly demolished to be replaced with retail outlets.

Below: It's not all that often that high-flying politicians visit Bury, except when a general election is in the air. In 1959, Harold Macmillan had only been in office for two years, with a further three to go, when he visited Bury. Accompanied by his wife, Lady Dorothy, the Prime Minister visited several Lancashire towns on the 24 and 25 April, 1959. He viewed the trip as "a most heartening experience" because of the large number of people in the streets to greet him. A British Conservative politician, he was Prime Minister from 1957 to 1963 and during that time earned the nickname of ' Supermac'. In this fabulous photograph he can be seen, along with Lady Dorothy, receiving a rousing send off as they leave a mill in Bury. One of the mill girls is wearing the traditional clogs and shawl. In earlier times, all mill women wore shawls and quite often they had inherited them from mothers or grandmothers. They wore them for everyday use and occasionally kept one for 'best' in a drawer.

Below: It is hard to imagine what the children in Lancashire would have made of this elderly Indian man, dressed in a loin cloth and wearing sandals. On the historic day, crowds had gathered to catch a glimpse of political leader, Mohandas Karamchand Gandhi (Mahatma), on his visit in September 1931. He had been invited to see the effects of his country's boycott of cotton goods by the owners of Greenfield Mill. Then aged 62, he was already in London for talks about the issue, when the opportunity arose to meet and speak to the unemployed workers from the Lancashire textile industry who had suffered because of the action. Gandhi was born on 2 October, 1869, in Porbandar, India. It is said he spoke English with an Irish accent, for one of his first teachers was an Irishman.

Right: This pair of leggy lovelies, looking very attractive in the fashionable hot pants that were all the rage in c1970, were helping advertise Hall's Mentho-lyptus tablets, a popular throat sweet and decongestant aid. The Lord Mayor's charity appeal was on a nationwide tour that summer and the vehicle by which the girls posed was a Fowler wagon, manufactured by a company based in Hunslet. No-one can be sure if the steam is coming from the boiler or out of the driver's ears, as he gazed upon the delightful view below.

Above: Stand still for a second, smile and say cheese, might have been the plea from this hopeful photographer. The kiddies were posing in their finery as they waited to take part in the Whit Sunday Walk in 1962. In some towns, walks might be held on a Friday or a Monday but the essence was still the same. Local churches were the centres of attention as congregations paraded behind banners, often accompanied by brass bands. Children had new clothes to wear and usually called round at relative's houses after the event, hoping to get something for their 'piggy bank'. Some grumpy uncle might complain that this was the only time in the year that his nephews and nieces showed their faces.

Right and below: The former Bury & Radcliffe Athletic Club sprint star Barrie Kelly (No 21) winning the AAAs championships at White City, London. Born in Bury on 2 August, 1940, Barrie Kelly became a world class athlete despite suffering from chronic asthma as a teenager and he didn't take up athletics until he was 22. In the 1960s and early 70s he had a glittering career, appearing in two Commonwealth Games, two European championships and the Mexico Olympics. Possibly his biggest success was in winning the 60 metres at the 1966 European Indoor Games, setting a British record in the semi-final. A testament to his commitment and determination he went on to represent Great Britain on 33 occasions, which was a record for a sprinter at that time and also captained the British men's team on several occasions. These days he is never happier than staying very, very still for long periods as he takes stunning photographs of birds and mammals from a dormouse to cheetahs.

Right: Two of the best we have ever seen, but a pair that is sadly lost, though not forgotten. On the right we see Alex Higgins, the twice world champion who was one of the finest natural talents snooker has ever seen. The player on the left is Radcliffe's John Spencer. Higgins and Spencer posed for a photograph before a challenge match in Bolton, not long after John became world champion for the first time. He repeated the feat in 1971 and again in 1977, being the first to lift the world crown at the Crucible in Sheffield. He was also the first to make a maximum 147 break in competition.

Right: This is a fabulous aerial view of our beloved Gigg Lane ground taken in 1965. The club was originally formed in 1885 by Aiden Arrowsmith following a meeting at the White Horse Hotel, between the Bury Wesleyans and Bury Unitarians Football Clubs. The first match to be played at Gigg Lane was a friendly between Bury and Wigan on 12 September, 1885, which Bury won 4–3. The first league game was a 4–2 victory over Manchester City on 8 September, 1894. Bury won the FA Cup on 21 April, 1900 they beat Southampton 4–0 in the FA Cup final at Crystal Palace, and returned to the London venue in 1903. The second win was achieved without conceding a goal in the entire competition, including a record FA Cup Final score of 6–0 over Derby County on 18 April, which remains the highest ever victory in an FA Cup Final. The capacity of the ground was once 35,000—and this capacity was reached when the record crowd was achieved for Bury's FA Cup third round tie against Bolton Wanderers on 9 January, 1960. The game ended 1–1 and Bury lost the replay after extra time 4–2.

Below: You would easily recognise the burly figure heading the football, if he had put on his more normal sporting apparel. The centre half is none other than Ian Botham, one of cricket's now knighted , who is arguably the best all-rounder to have played that game. Although batting and bowling were his main forte, Botham was no fool on the soccer field. Here he is seen playing for Scunthorpe United against Bury, at the Old Showground, in the second round of the FA Cup in December 1983. We lost 2-0 and Scunthorpe went on to beat Leeds in the next round.

Right: After playing for Northern Nomads, Craig Madden began his professional career at Bury in 1977. He spent nine years as a striker at Gigg Lane, making almost 300 league appearances and scoring 129 goals as a Shaker. He still holds the record for the most goals (43) in the 1981-82 season (35 league & 8 Cup).

A sporting record was achieved In August 2005, when Bury became first and still only club to score 1000 goals in all four professional tiers in England.

AROUND THE TOWN

The elongated lines of some of our cars in the swinging 60s aped the American sedans as a lot of us turned our gaze across the 'big pond' for ideas in fashion and style. However, if you wanted good taste then our Transatlantic cousins could come to us and enjoy the architectural delights our Art Gallery could offer both on the outside and within its galleries. Known as Bury Art Museum since 2011, it was officially opened by the Earl of Derby in October 1901. Initially, it was inaugurated to house the Wrigley Collection: oil paintings, watercolours, prints and ceramics accumulated by a local paper manufacturer.

Right: Barclays Bank cut an imposing architectural figure in our town centre in the 1960s. Situated at 26 Silver Street, its very style suggested that pinstripes were essential garb for anyone seeking employment here. There was certainly no chance of a silly, dress down Friday. Dealing with financial matters was far too important for such frippery. Anyway, how could you entrust your cash to a counter clerk in a Hawaiian shirt? The building came into being in 1868 for use by the Bury Banking Company, originally founded in 1778 as Grundy and Wood. The upper floor was once used as Bury's Council Chambers. It became the Lancashire and Yorkshire Bank in 1888, Martin's 40 years later and Barclays another 40 years after that. This branch closed in 2010 and relocated to The Rock.

Below: The Temperance Bar on the left was something of a Lancastrian anachronism as it seemed to be that our county was almost on its own in promoting such establishments in the 19th and early 20th centuries. At first, they recommended moderation in alcohol consumption, but later moved on to total abstinence in just offering for sale such beverages as dandelion and burdock, cream soda, ginger beer, Vimto and sarsaparilla. The temperance movement was very popular with Methodists and members of the Salvation Army. They preached about the evils of demon drink and, with so many families' lives ruined by meagre finances being metaphorically poured down people's throats, who could argue with them? To the right of the bar in the picture, you can make out an advert for Craven "A" cigarettes, which were hugely popular during World War II. Smoking was permitted and accepted in most public places. It was quite normal to be stopped in the street and asked if one had a light - presumably because the individual concerned had run out of matches or petrol for his or her lighter. At that time, no-one seemed concerned at being approached by a perfect stranger if he or she was a fellow smoker.

Above: A ground level view of the photograph on page 52, that has also been used as the image for the front page of this book. The car waiting at the crossing on the Haymarket has the look of a Mark II version of the Rover P5, 3-Litre which was introduced in 1962. Above the heads of the people crossing we can see part of the chimney to the School of Arts and Crafts. Serving the boiler house, the 100ft high chimney was designed by local architect Maxwell Tuke. He gained national fame in 1895 with his slightly bigger 520ft Blackpool Tower. On the right is the entrance to the landscaped Kay Gardens, an open space created from the former market place when a new market hall was built in 1901.

Above: A lone cyclist rides towards the camera in this photograph looking along The Rock in 1954. Behind the cameraman is Union Street and looking forward to Moorgate, in the distance. On the right, we can see the steel framed Hornby buildings which were built in 1933 by Bury Corporation and named after a former landowner. Further along Entwhistle's are promoting the fact that they were established 100 years ago, back in the 1850s. On the left is Saxone Shoes, who have been a common site on the High Street for years. We would love to believe the myth that chain gets its name from a shock football result many decades ago, when Kilmarnock (of whom the Scottish founder was a keen supporter) beat Glasgow Rangers 6-1 (in Scots, sax-one) The shop name pronunciation has changed now to 'sax-own'.

Left: This long straight stretch of the A56 Manchester Road seems unusually quiet in this photograph from the mid-1950s. The shot was taken looking northwards towards Bury, in the Fishpool area. Off to the left is Radcliffe Road and Parkshills Road is to the right. The pedestrian crossing is outside the Staff of Life public house at the junction with Heaton Fold. The pub is traditionally busy when Bury F.C. are at home as it is the nearest pub to the Gigg Lane ground. Today the ornate facia of the building is still in evidence but the crossing has disappeared, to be replaced by traffic lights. Just past the Staff of Life are the Pack Horse Hotel and the shops alongside, which were built by John Ward from Leigh, who was at one time landlord of the Church Inn on Spring Street.

The setts on the Haymarket have been replaced by a tarmac surface to the roadway, but the Belisha crossing is still there alongside Kay Gardens. When photographed in 1963, we were enjoying trips into town to see some of the best movies ever released. We could choose from The Great Escape, Cleopatra, From Russia with Love, Pink Panther and The Birds. On our way home we could sing to ourselves such memorable hits as She Loves You, How Do You Do It and Summer Holiday. Those examples are exactly what we mean about 'the good old days', so do not let youngsters try to convince you that The Revenant is worth watching or that Kanye West deserves to command so much as one ear of attention.

The men sitting on the benches in Kay Gardens in 1958 looked across Haymarket Street to the grandly titled Bury Shopping Centre. Our grandchildren would smirk today at such a title for this little bank of shops when they have such large malls and superstores in which they can fritter away their inflated pocket money today. The old centre is still there, next to the Knowsley Hotel, but the shops are uninspiring, containing a number of fast food outlets of the pizza and curry type.

In this pair of images we are looking at The Rock in 1958. The picture below shows Crompton Street to the right and was taken from a spot just outside St Mary's Church. The chemist on the corner was a famous name from that period. Timothy White opened a general store in Portsmouth in 1848, before turning to pharmacy. Within 40 years he had built up a chain of such outlets. A merger in 1935 brought about the Timothy White and Taylor title. The company was taken over by Boot's in 1968 and the Timothy White name mothballed in 1985. The companion picture above shows Williams Deacon's Bank, on the corner of Gutter End. The building remains as the Royal Bank of Scotland, but the premises owned by Downham's ironmongery business was swept away and replaced by Mothercare.

This part of the Bury District Co-operative building is seen not long after it opened in these premises in 1952. By then co-operatives were over 100 years old, having first seen the light of day as a small undertaking in a shop on Toad Lane, Rochdale in 1844. Those of us with long memories will recall saving up our dividend or 'divvy' that we received as customers and shareholders. This was seen as something central to the fabric of British life and, at its peak in the mid 1950s, the Co-op had a 20% share of the food and 12% share of the non-food retail markets.

In the post-war period, there was a major decline in the cotton industry, and in common with many neighbouring towns, Bury's skyline was to become very different, with countless factory chimneys being pulled down and the associated mills closing their doors for ever. In this photograph from the early 1960s, we can still see over a dozen chimneys belching out smoke above the Bury skyline. In the foreground is the abattoir on Knowsley Street which first opened for business in 1903. Cattle were brought in by truck and rail from special sidings at Knowsley Street Station. The slaughterhouse was at the rear of the building. For people living within the vicinity of the building the smell was unforgettable. It closed in 1972 and the site was cleared for a car park. The two ornamental lions on the gable were preserved and relocated to Bury Lions' Garden. The distinctive dome of the old market and the white facade of the Bury Co-op building stand out in the background on Market Street.

An elderly gentleman dressed in his raincoat and flat cap, strolls across the crossing in this picture from 1968, between the tallest Belisha beacons ever seen. It is interesting that this photograph was probably taken around the time of the devastating fire that destroyed the old indoor market hall. The dome on the left, remained largely in tact during the fire, but from the normality of the photograph it is fair to assume that this was an earlier scene. Looking along the right hand side of Market Street we can see the well known Queen's Hotel and just next door, the recognisable Bury Co-op building. Further along, looking towards Market Place the many windowed curved building is still the same today, opposite the entrance to the Millgate Shopping Centre.

This rooftop view of Bury market hall was captured just prior to a devastating fire in November 1968, when the building was razed to the ground. The building with the dome in the centre of this image is the covered market. This would have been on of the last photographs of this outlook before the building was destroyed. Clearly this is market

day judged by the crowds in the open-air section of the market. Inn the background we can just make out the white walls of the Co-op Emporium and the top of the Queen's Hotel next door. Smaller shops now occupy the curved building, looking out towards the 'New' Interchange.

Below: This elevated view looks across the 'Square', which was once the vibrant hub of the town. In this photograph from 1964, we can see work has already begun on the concrete precinct built to replace the old shopping area and housing around Union Square and Princess Street. At one time the area was a very up-market residential location in Bury, the home of important mill owners, preofessional people and civic leaders. Wartime Bury, saw the 'Square' dug up to accommodate massive air-raid shelters which could take up to 700 people in the event of a German bombing raid. In more recent times it was known as the home of Casewell's the internationally renowned black pudding manufacturer, who operated from nearby Spring Street. In the 1990s the development in this area was replaced by the Mill Gate Shopping Centre. This development was replaced by the Mill Gate Shopping Centre in the late 1990s. But now the name of Union Square has been selected for the new public square at Knowsley Place, opposite Bury Town Hall.

Right: The red and white pole outside James Edward Blakemore's Ladies & Gents hairdressers shop, is a link with a time gone by. During medieval times, barbers performed surgery on customers, as well as tooth extractions. However, today's barber poles represent little more than being a barber shop that shaves and cuts hair. Established in 1906, the premises are still used for men's and boys hairdressing today. Posters outside the Evening Chronicle office next door, advertise a wide variety of newspaper topics from 'Tommy Weston's Turf Secrets', to a story about 'Stalin's Secret Life'. It is hard to believe, but the photograph was taken just before Christmas almost 60 years ago. The newspaper names etched on the shop window are a throwback to this era. In 1955 the Daily Dispatch merged with the News Chronicle, which was subsequently absorbed into the Daily Mail in 1960. The Evening Chronicle merged with the Manchester Evening News in 1963.

A delightful photograph for vintage car enthusiasts with a mixture of makes from the 1930s and 1940s, including Austin and Wolseley. The are parked outside the familiar landmark of Downham's Ironmongery and Furnishers on Union Street, around 1950. The camera is pointing in the direction of The Rock in days before this road was made one-way. In the post-war period, there was a major decline in the cotton industry, and in common with many neighbouring towns, Bury's commercial centre was soon very different. The old shopping area around Princess Street and Union Square was demolished in the late 1960s, and a concrete precinct emerged to replace it. This development was replaced by the Mill Gate Shopping Centre in the late 1990s.

Unbelievably this photograph of Kay Gardens was taken over 60 years ago, in an age where the pace of life seemed much slower and more relaxed. Many features shown here combine to rekindle fond memories of the way the area used to look. Before the age of pedestrianisation, buses used to drive past the Co-op building, and shelters lined the triangular pathways around the immaculately kept gardens. Many of the older generation are enjoying a seat in the summer sunshine. The gardens and monument were first opened in April 1908, on the site of Lord Derby's 1839 market, following the building of a new market hall in 1901. The gardens and monument were commissioned and paid for by Henry Whitehead, a local mill owner. Kay Monument is Grade II Listed and a tribute to John Kay who was born in Bury in 1704 and was most famous in Lancashire as the inventor of 'The Flying Shuttle'. The monument was designed by Bristol architect William Venn Gough who had become known in Bury through his work on the Grammar School.

DISTRICT CO OPERATIVE SOCIETY LTD

WHEN WE WERE YOUNG

Holy Cross School was started as long ago as 1887 when Cardinal Vaughan welcomed some of the teachers of the Belgium Congregation of Daughter of the Cross, who had recently been banished from Germany, to the Bury area. The facilities were very meagre, but from a small base and charging a penny a week, the school began to grow. Several moves along he Manchester Road saw the school enter larger premises at The Ferns, part of todays college. Only two years before this photo was taken the school had ceased being a public primary school and became a secondary school. Here we see seven staff in charge of around 28, very well presented young ladies. The walls are decorated with ferns, flowers, pictures and antler horns, no doubt to generate discussion topics. It is a wonderful scene of the early twentieth century academic system in Bury.

Below: This is a mixed group of youngsters playing on the climbing frame and swings in the very early 1900s. Some are well dressed, with breeches, boots and caps, whilst others go bare-footed. The girl at the centre of the picture with the light coloured dress and wide brimmed bonnet seems to be attracting the attention of most of the boys, whilst the little ones scramble precariously above them. Its also nice to see what is possibly the oldest lad in the group bending down to encourage the little girl with her wild mop of blonde hair, to look at the camera. So playground climbing frames are nothing new and the forward thinking council of Bury saw the need for parks, recreation and play areas.

Right: Hollymount School continues as a well respected school for the children of Bury and can be seen from this photo to be ahead of its time as far back as 1910. The children here are seen enjoying a tea party and all look very well behaved with no teacher in sight but we are guessing he or she is just out of shot. The little tots to the left do indeed look like babies but older children are also present in the classroom which is well adorned with a dolls house, paintings and posters. Built in the 1860s as a College for Young Gentlemen it had to close in 1885, reopening in 1888 as a Covent and Poor School and has since been an orphanage, retirement home and cared for injured soldiers during the war. But these well behaved youngsters would not be aware of the history of school just interested in any cakes and jelly that may be available at such a special tea party.

The occasion was the 50th anniversary of Bury's Charter of Incorporation received in 1876, creating the town as a Municipal Borough and the people of Bury were looking to celebrate this jubilee in style. None more so than Mr W Morgan who arranged for over 7000 children to be transported on trams to the Wellington Playing Fields. As we can see from the photo, the children were organised to create an image of the Bury Coat of Arms. The emblem displays elements of each the areas of Bury with an anvil and fleece at the top and shuttles and papyrus plant at the bottom. The day was a great success and turned out to be even better when the Mayor, Councillor Hartley, announced that the children could have an extra day off school in the holidays. Bury became a County Borough in 1888 and was later brought into the Greater Manchester in 1974 much to the annoyance of many 'Burmunians'.

Left: Cars, tractors and horses any would do as long as they kept going around and around. These youngsters at Bury Fair in the 1960s were happy enough on this kiddies roundabout, they hadn't yet reached the age where a large Ferris Wheel of noisy Dodgems would be the place to be at any fair. Mums and dads were happy enough to watch their little ones and a more sedate ride for the time being. The Carousel with its galloping horses has entertained crowds at fairgrounds since the reign of Queen Victoria. A scaled down version of the most popular fairground attraction of all time. The kid's carousel is an eye catching centrepiece for event and the young children are patiently waiting for their turn.

Right: The roads had been a little quieter in the early 1950s due to petrol shortages, war time mileage restrictions and shortages of parts. This had all meant it was a better experience for the cyclists on the road. However, this was not going to last and with more cars beginning to use the roads, cyclist safety became a real priority. Accident statistics particularly amongst the young cyclists, were alarming. The National Cycling Proficiency scheme was therefore launched. It took place in school playgrounds and car parks helped on through willing adult volunteers. To prove that you had listened and understood a practical and oral test would be take and if successful you would receive a certificate and that triangular badge you must remember. We wonder if Jacqueline Sandford seen here was successful that day.

Right: A somewhat informal example of maypole dancing taking place in May, 1960. Though half the folk around today seem to imagine that the May Day bank holiday has something to do with celebrating the Russian Revolution, or perhaps the birth of Karl Marx, nothing could be further from the truth. May Day is an ancient pagan fertility festival, later co-opted and tolerated by the Christian church. Maypole dancing took place in most neighbourhoods each year on 1 May, with a May Queen being chosen from among local girls. And what excitement and jealously that could raise, with mothers convinced beyond reason that their disappointed daughters were the ones that really had the strongest claim to the throne. The overt symbolism, obvious in previous centuries, was long lost by the 20th century to be replaced by a gentle and civilised folk custom which delighted everyone involved in the annual celebrations.

Left: When we were younger, children had to use their imagination to create play situations. Throughout the war most children played with toys that were either handed down from friends or relatives, or that were homemade. In the 1940s post-war period the effects of war-time rationing remained present in British attitudes. Waste was not an option. After the war people continued to recycle, reuse and repair items, including clothes and toys. These children had heard from their older siblings about seeking out salvage during the war, so they put that experience to good use in peacetime. They foraged for stuff discarded from local shops. They can be seen in this image from 1948, making off with Jubbly ice boxes and a 'Players please' sign. As Del Boy would say...'Lovely Jubbly!'.

Below: Perhaps Enid Blyton could have used this scene as an inspiration for a new series of books. If she had, then instead of the Famous Five or Secret Seven, there might have been the Tremendous Ten. The nine children, along with Mick the dog, were having a whale of a time on the see-saw, precariously perched on several blocks of stone. No doubt their mums had warned them that it would all end in tears, but youngsters need to take a few risks and experience the odd scraped knee in order to mature. They need to be protected, but not cosseted. So what, if they came down to earth with a bump as they could dust themselves off and start all over again.

Below: Summer holidays were an idyllic time for children in the Bury area. School was over and it was time for playing and just messing about with friends, and younger brothers, if they behaved. These two young chaps are John and Luke Wheeldon, are having a great time on their parents farm near Bury. Later in their teens they would help mum and dad out with the heavy farm work and rearing pigs and cows. But for now it was play time and having such a fine racing car to peddle around in, albeit having to pull little brother along in a home made trailer, was always much better than sitting down at a school desk to learn the three R's. By the looks of the front offside wheel, a bit of maintenance could be need before too long.

This was 'Harts Travelling Fair' which was one of many fairs to visit Bury over the decades and this photo provides a good view of the attractions available to the public in the 1960s. It was definitely the place to be and we can see the Dodgems, Big Wheel, Waltzer and that looks like Mitchell's Speedway circular track, with the high sides panels at the rear. It is very quiet so the shot was probably taken on a morning after morning the excitement of the previous night.

Children young and old enjoyed the thrill of the fair, with all the noise and loud music, candy floss and toffee apples. The Royal Huntsman Hotel in the distance was a popular Thwaites hotel, which succumbed to the modernisation of Bury in the 1980s and was demolished in 1985.

Below: Wow, nearly got that one', as two you lads battle it out in Bury. As the conkers fell off the horse chestnut trees in the autumn, boys would select the firm ones and drill a hole in them for the string and then soak the conker in vinegar or bake it, to make it hard. There was a lot of effort put into first getting and keeping a good conker. The challenge was taken and the game was played in pairs, the idea was to swing your conker to hit the opponent's one. The game ended when one conker got broken. Then the unbroken conker was declared the 'winner', rather than the owner. If done strategically you might be able to smash another five conkers, and yours would then be known as a 'fiver' and become the target for your mates to beat.

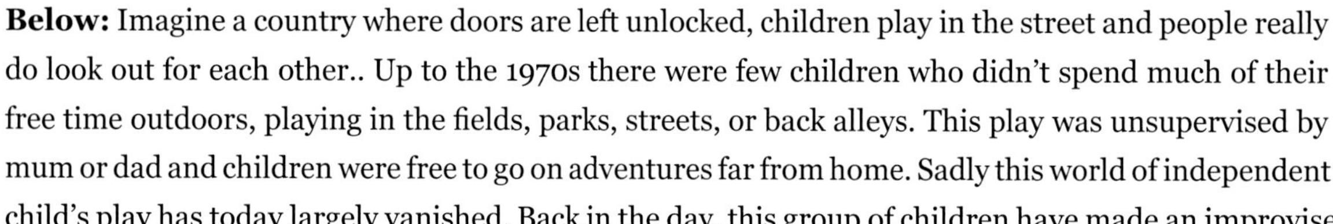

Below: Imagine a country where doors are left unlocked, children play in the street and people really do look out for each other.. Up to the 1970s there were few children who didn't spend much of their free time outdoors, playing in the fields, parks, streets, or back alleys. This play was unsupervised by mum or dad and children were free to go on adventures far from home. Sadly this world of independent child's play has today largely vanished. Back in the day, this group of children have made an improvised tyre swing hanging from a tree branch. In an age before satellite TV andvideo games, children were happy to play outside all day, no matter how hot or cold it was. Many people think children today spend too much time in front of the telly or the computer, and not enough time playing outdoors. We didn't have mobile phones and iPads, but we got a lot of fun out of simple stuff, like climbing trees, hide and seek, and things like that.

Above: It doesn't look as if it started life as a reservoir but the Clarence Lido off Milner Avenue was just that. It did need a bit of an upgrade though, so in 1963 and £14000 later the Lido was completed. It was something of a triumph for the local council and they were rightly pleased about what they considered to be the 'finest Lido in the north'. The Lido was officially opened on 13 May, 1987 by the then Mayor Councillor J Roberts and Mayoress Mrs A Roberts. This scene looks like a very warm sunny day in Bury as the lads sat on the steps seem to be comfortable enough in their swimming trunks and even those on the platoon continue to brave the water. It was a major improvement for Bury's Recreation Grounds and was hoped to attract tourists and day trippers and maybe it did if the weather stayed warm.

Left: Dating from the late 1930s this scene will bring back memories, not just for those who were children in that hungry decade, but also for those who were young for many decades afterwards. The classic 'witch's hat' roundabout was a feature of children's playgrounds until the 1970s, when the design fell foul of elf 'n' safety officials who deemed them too dangerous for youngsters to play on. Well maybe they were a little bit dangerous, but they were certainly great fun: get a gang of big boys all round, and the entire thing could be lifted off its mounting. And of course the witch's hat didn't just go round and round – the design meant it could swing at same time. True, some accidents did occur, but it did not put the children off from coming back again and again!

Right: We don't know who this little chap is, but we do know he was probably an evacuee from on of the larger cities. At the start of the Second World War, in 1939, German bombing was expected to quickly devastate cities such as London and Leeds, Liverpool and Manchester. In response to that threat the Government arranged for many thousands of children to be evacuated, sent to safety, to live with families in more rural parts of Britain. This young chap is one of them. Not every household forced to have strange children billeted on them was happy with the arrangement; and many evacuees had horror stories to tell. But this evacuee at least looks happy enough with a hoop to play with. The young fellow is wearing clogs, still at that time familiar everyday footwear for many people.

Above: If you heard the chimes of the ice cream van coming down the street playing greensleeves, you would need to check if you had any pocket money left, or see if your mum was in a really good mood. It looks like these kids were fortunate and were queuing for their favourite treat. Now then would it be a cornet with raspberry sauce drizzled on top or a ninety-nine with a chocolate flake. Well-known brands of ice lollies produced by Lyons Maid included, Zoom, Strawberry Mivvi, Orange Maid and Fab. You hope that the little lad on the grass will not be left out and that a brother or sister will be getting something for him.

GETTING FROM A TO B

It looks like a still from a Laurel and Hardy or Charlie Chaplin movie, but this was no comedy. Here we have serious motoring, 1899 style. The first car seen in town was supplied by Hargreaves and Sons for Councillor Walter Ashworth. At the time, this was state of the art technology and was regarded as something bordering on the miraculous that man could drive around town in what was known as a 'horseless carriage'. Such vehicles may be amusing period pieces to us today, but in Victorian Britain they were wonders of the age.

Below: The tram heading for Moorside had just passed the Swan Hotel on Tottington Road. It was one of the first of the fleet of public transport vehicles to be electrically powered and was still something of a novelty in the early 1900s. The Tramways Company sent out horse drawn vehicles in the 1880s, starting with a service to Blackford Bridge, and these were in operation for another 20 years. But, Edwardian England saw huge advances in the way we moved about, both on the ground and in the air. Motorised machines, now known as cars, buses and trams, were powered by petrol or electricity, carrying us quickly and, for the most part reliably, whilst the marvel of aviation was demonstrated in the skies above.

Below: Jericho in Israel is believed to be one of the oldest cities in the world, but in this case is a district to the east of Bury on the road out to Rochdale. It is also on the tram service route that was the first to be electrified in 1903. The vehicle pictured offered a draughty ride for passengers who ventured onto the top deck and the open driver's cab did not offer the most pleasant of working conditions, but needs must and these trams continued in service for several years. Eventually common sense and comfort prevailed and the top deck was covered and the cab enclosed. It is thought that the district got its Biblical name because John Wesley preached there in 1778 about walls coming tumbling down in one of his fire and brimstone sermons.

The evocative photographs on these two pages are a nostalgic reminder of days gone by and a trainspotters dream. They are a celebratory reminder to those who are known as "ferroequinologists" (students of iron horses). Trainspotting had been regarded as a largely 20th century activity, beginning with the publication of E Nesbit's The Railway Children in 1906, and peaking in the Fifties and Sixties, before the country's last mainline steam train service stopped in 1968. Schoolboys in caps, short trousers and knee-length socks would gaze up in awe at the great piston-churning beasts. Their rucksacks and shoulder bags often held packed lunches and Thermos flasks to sustain them through long hours spent patiently waiting.

It was recently announced that evidence had been discovered of what is thought to be the earliest ever proponent of the hobby: a 14-year-old girl named Fanny Johnson, who kept a notebook of the locomotives roaring through London's Westbourne Park in 1861.

Left: It does your heart good to see a steam train in all its glory. Sadly for those of us who used to enjoy the thrill of listening to the roar of heavy machinery, as the express thundered through a station, or the fun of ducking below a bridge's parapets to avoid being enveloped in white clouds belching from its boiler, those days belong to yesteryear. Of course, we who live in or around Bury can still enjoy the delights of steam locomotion thanks to the East Lancashire Railway that provides services on the 12 mile heritage line from Heywood to Rawtenstall.

Right: This delightful scene was captured at Bolton Street Station on a Sunday in September 1957. The Class 5 locomotive is about to leave for Manchester Victoria via Clifton Junction. The 15.20 from Colne is in the up-bay platform. It is amazing to think that the original East Lancashire Railway station has been in use since 1846, when it was known as Bury Station and linked Manchester to Radcliffe and Bury. The station was renamed Bury Bolton Street in February 1866.

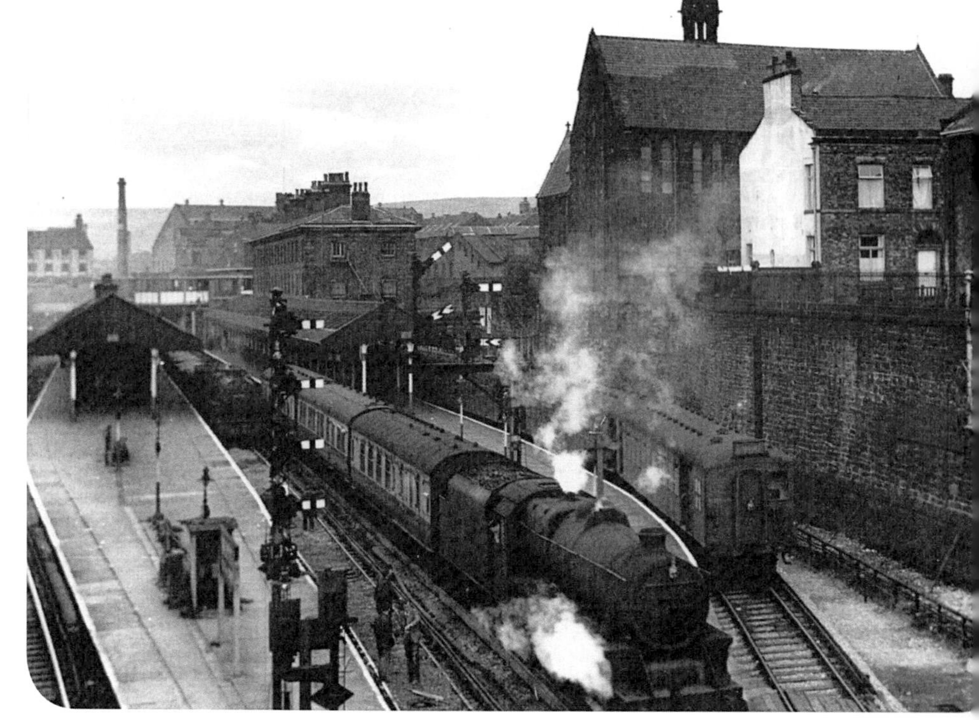

Above: This fabulous image from 1963 depicts a steam locomotive and carriages approaching Bolton Street Station. The railway was to play an important part in supporting local industry and even carried thousands of factory workers to northern seaside resorts for their annual Wakes Week holiday. In this case this is a more modest Bury Knowsley Street to Blackpool half day excursion.

Right: This is a different view of the town as locomotive number 48437 approaches Bolton Street Station in 1963. The goods train is the 17.10 Nelson-Moston class D, we are reliably informed. The Railway Age came to Bury in the years between 1840 and 1860. It is difficult looking back, particularly for younger readers, to comprehend the massive impact that the railways had upon local industry and the lives of ordinary people.

Thankfully today as you pass through the remarkable 1950s visage of our Bury Bolton Street Station you would be forgiven for thinking you had taken a step back in time. The reassuring rumble and roar of passing locomotives, the satisfying hiss and the pleasant smell of banks of steam rolling along the platform, the welcoming cry and whistle of the train guard signaling the beginning of another grand adventure.

The East Lancashire Railway is an immaculately preserved slice of British history, spanning a twelve mile route through magnificent Lancashire scenery.

Below: This single decker bus was in use just after the last war. It had been as late as 1925 when the Corporation first introduced motor buses, by opening a service to Walshaw. The decision to abandon trams was taken in 1933, though not fully implemented until after the war, but this still meant that buses were seen as the future for public transport in our town. The one we have here was destined to make the journey to Nangreaves, a name derived from the Saxon for a goatherd. The village grew in size largely thanks to John Hall who built a mill at Mount Pleasant in the early 19th century. It was still in use until the early 1980s, but was destroyed by a fire later that decade.

Right: In the days before children were driven to school by yummy mummies in 4 x 4s, we either walked there or took a bus like the Leyland seen on Knowsley Street in the mid 1950s. Once on board we could play games with our pals, such as identifying the registration area of a vehicle by reading its number plate. The bus was easy, as 'EN' meant Bury. We collected roll ends from ticket machines and argued about whether or not Horwich's Gordon Atherton was the best right half outside the First Division. We competed to count the most legs suggested by pub names and argued about the total that the Coach and Horses should score.

Above: The scene is definitely one from the late 1960s. The buildings are all featureless mixtures of glass and concrete, boringly constructed in rectangular shapes without a gargoyle, cupola or raised relief in sight. This single decker was manufactured by Daimler and one of the Roadliner models that introduced step free access for passengers long before most of its rivals. This made it popular with elderly passengers tired of 'minding the step'. It was produced between 1962 and 1972, but was notoriously unreliable and often had transmission problems.

BREAD & CAKES
NORMAN'S
TRANSPORT LTD.
PHONES
FAILSWORTH 4091/2
Carriers for
Prestige
Prestige
GEN 419

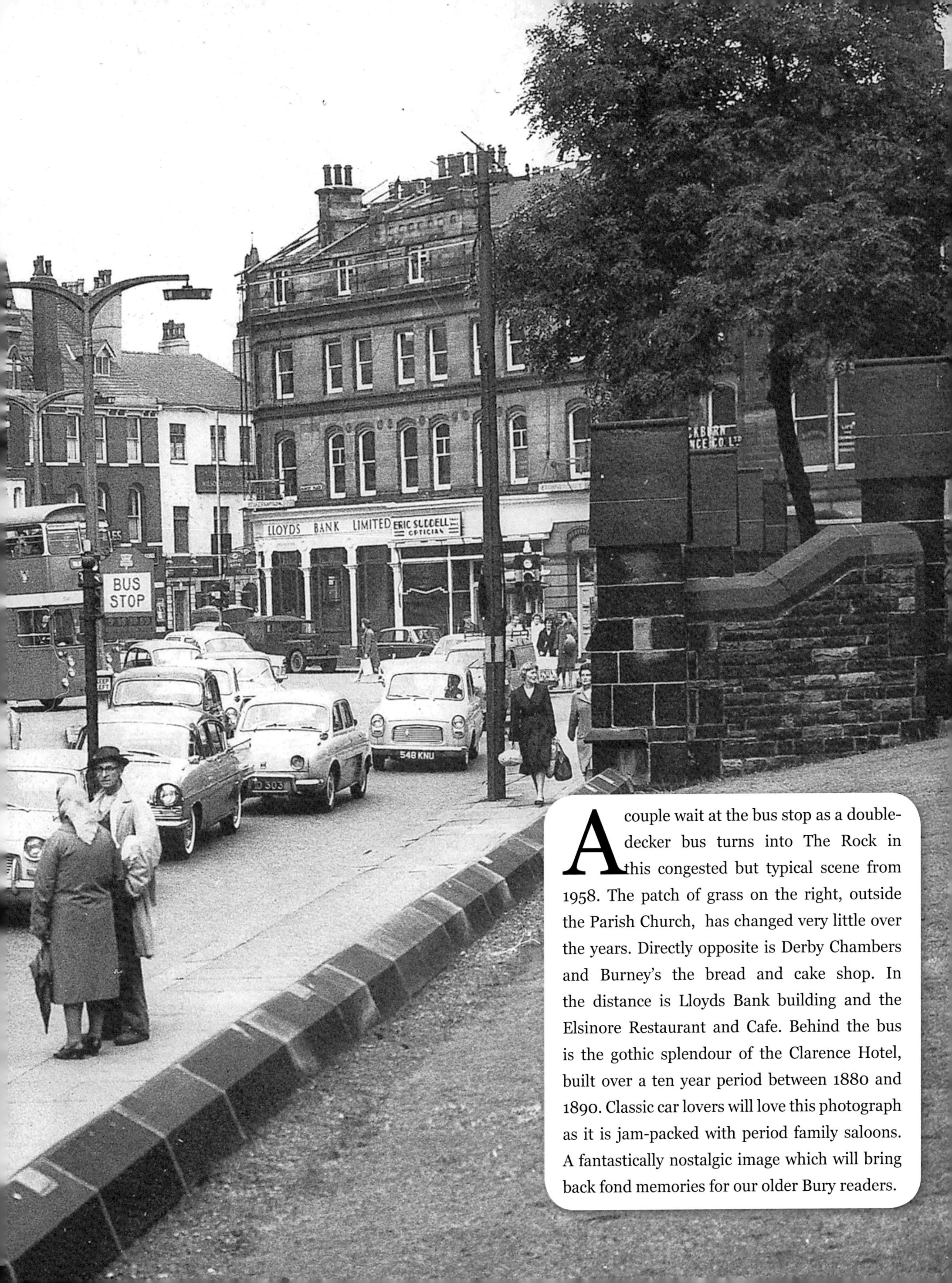

A couple wait at the bus stop as a double-decker bus turns into The Rock in this congested but typical scene from 1958. The patch of grass on the right, outside the Parish Church, has changed very little over the years. Directly opposite is Derby Chambers and Burney's the bread and cake shop. In the distance is Lloyds Bank building and the Elsinore Restaurant and Cafe. Behind the bus is the gothic splendour of the Clarence Hotel, built over a ten year period between 1880 and 1890. Classic car lovers will love this photograph as it is jam-packed with period family saloons. A fantastically nostalgic image which will bring back fond memories for our older Bury readers.

Below: In 1951, the Stanley Arms, on The Rock, was a Walker's house. This was a Warrington brewery founded in 1864, merging with Robert Cain's in 1921. It became part of the Tetley empire in 1960. Now one of Bury's lost drinking spots, the featured pub owes its title to the Earls of Derby as Stanley is their family name. The bus heading our way was one of the Ribble Motor Services fleet. The company was founded in 1919 and it grew to dominate public transport from Carlisle down to south Lancashire. Its head offices were in Preston.

Right: We hardly needed the labelling on the lead Scammell Contractor truck making its way along the road at Holcombe Brook to tell us that this was 'heavy transport'. The firm of Econofreight was a specialist in the heavy heaulage sector. This would be classed by the firm as a 'heavy' haul but not an 'extreme' weight that the company built its reputation on. The 150 tonne cylinder was on its way from the Beloit foundry in Bolton to Stubbins Mill, Ramsbottom where it would be used in the paper tissue manufacturing process. Owned at the time by the Georgia-Pacific Corporation, the company passed into the hands of SCA Hygiene Products in 2012.

Right: It was getting crowded on Haymarket Street in the early 1960s when this photograph was taken. Several of the cars we see were typical of this period of motoring as they had names we can still easily recall today. Ford Cortina, Ford Anglia and Morris Minor are part and parcel of our driving heritage. Although we cannot see one here, throw in a BMC Mini and you probably have a set. Car ownership really took off apace during the swinging 60s. We were all much better off than in the immediate postwar austerity years and family saloons appeared in abundance on many driveways in the land. Some readers might recall HW Sly's jewellers, a prestigious retail outlet at 2-4 Haymarket Street. Clocks, watches and other items bearing the Sly name often now command good prices at auction or on eBay.

WORK, INDUSTRY & COMMERCE

Above: At the end of the First World War, Prime Minister David Lloyd George promised us a 'land fit for heroes'. He forgot to mention that we would have to bend our backs and work flat out to achieve it. Here men laid tram tracks along a section of Walmersley Road from Limefield to the New Inn, where the Mulberry Bush Nursery can now be found. Steam powered trams had been around in Bury since 1883, and electric trams had been employed since 1903. Public transport methods were changing however and less than ten years after this scene was captured the end of the tramway era was heralded by the introduction of motorbuses.

Right: Inspired by James Watt, Joseph Webb founded a small steam powered iron rolling mill in the Midlands. He saw the chance for expansion by moving to Lancashire in 1846 and manufacturing rolled iron bars and associated metal products for use in the textile industry. After his death, the company, based in its forge and wharf at Bury Bridge, passed into the hands of his sons, Henry and George. The former also became a JP and helped found the Girls' Grammar School. George spread his wings by setting up the Bury Coffee House Company. Life in the foundry was a hot and dirty affair, as can be seen in this photograph dating from 1935. Still, at least these men had employment as the 1930s was that dreadful time known as the 'Great Depression' when families struggled to make ends meet.

Above: We can see from the streamers and bunting that a celebration was about to take place at Warth Mills in Bury. The occasion was the Coronation of Her Majesty Queen Elizabeth II in June 1953. After the misery endured during the war this was one of the first national events to really capture the hearts of the ordinary people. 'Now Let The Trumpets Sound' was the front page headline in Northern Daily Telegraph. Bunting, balloons and street parties helped mark the royal occasion for cheering townsfolk across villages throughout Lancashire and across the UK. Warth Mill was formerly Mellor's Mill and had a long association with the cotton industry. The mill was constructed in the 1860s by Colonel John James Mellor, the youngest of 15 children. His contribution to Bury life was such that he had Mellor Hall and Mellor treet named after him. During the Second World War the government requisitioned the property for use as a wartime prison for German and Italian prisoners.

Mill working has been central to the lives of countless thousands of Bury people for generations. The picture here is the interior at one of James Kenyon and Son's mills, on Derby Street. The largely female workforce are taking a break from the hard work and incessant noise to pose for a photograph. The Union flag bunting suggest this is part of the celebrations linked to the Coronation of Queen Elizabeth II, in 1953. James Kenyon and Son, cotton spinners and manufacturers, had several mill properties throughout the district and were a major local employer. The company can trace its roots back to 1714, making it one of the oldest cotton enterprises in the north. These hard working employees represent several generations and no doubt each would have a fascinating story to tell about life in the mill.

Right: Adverting Hargreaves's products was not so much hot air as fresh air. The company was a long established local firm that specialised in ventilation ductwork and associated items. Here one of its vans was sitting inside a shaft built in 1954 for use in the mining industry. Henry Hargreaves was born in 1851 and became a time-served tinsmith before founding his own company in Bury in 1872. By 1890, it had become the family firm of Hargreaves and Sons and it acquired a workshop in Heywood Street, Bury where the manufacture of loaf tins and lawnmower boxes was undertaken. Shortly afterwards, premises were opened in Silver Street, selling bicycles. About this time, the first roof ventilators used on churches and schools were manufactured. It was this aspect of work that would be the focus from then onward.

Right: Blimey, shine a light! It is not just the Motor Show at the NEC that thinks it is a good idea to use glamorous models to help advertise its wares. This light fittings store in Bury decided that it could also attract custom by giving its shop window that bit extra in the way of adornment. Liz Wood donned a bikini and enjoyed the winter sunshine streaming through the pane. The view from the other side of the glass certainly lit up the morning for the chap pictured out on the street.

Above: Eat your heart out, Mary Berry! There were plenty of people around before you and your pals came along with TV programmes about how to bake pastries or get a rise out of a soufflé. Bernard Slattery (centre), along with his wife, Margaret, opened a bakery in Crumpsall in 1967. They made everything, from the humblest buns to the most elaborate of wedding cakes. The photograph shows Bernard and his colleagues busy piping decorations. Their children were introduced into the business as time went by and other outlets around Greater Manchester were opened.

Thousands of Bury folk will recognise this image of shop floor workers at the Hall Bros factory, having been employed by the company over the years. Local brothers Norman Smith Hall and Thomas Harold Hall founded the business in 1893. In 1927 the company began manufacturing Halls Mentholyptus cough drops, from the factory in Stanley Road, Whitefield. The product became the world's best known, best selling cough drop. By the mid 1960s Halls' products accounted for about a third of the UK market for medicated sweets. The factory moved to Dumers Lane Radcliffe in 1969.

Wallwork Heat Treatment Ltd

Firm's long and proud history

This thriving heat treatment business was founded by Robert Wallwork in 1959. The Wallwork family had a long history of being involved in engineering in Manchester, including the operation of a large foundry in Red Bank, Manchester.

Initially, Wallwork Heat Treatment had premises in Mersey Square, Stockport, and then Knowl Street, in Stalybridge, before the move to Bury. The original Lodge Bank Works chimney bearing the lettering 'B & J 1878' was eventually demolished in the late 1980s.

The company carries out heat treatment of metal components for the manufacturing industry, anything from kitchen knives to large gears for marine gearboxes. More recently, it has specialised in processing aircraft components and aero engine parts.

wallwork

Metal processing and engineering have long been associated with Bury so when Wallwork Heat Treatment was looking for new premises in 1979, Lodge Bank Works in Lord Street made an ideal new home.

The buildings had originally been used by Bentley and Jackson - founded in 1860 - to manufacture paper making machinery. They afforded the good headroom and overhead cranes that Wallwork needed to allow the installation of large heat treatment furnaces.

Wallwork has operated a fleet of distinctive bright green trucks since the mid-1970s (long before Asda started to use the colour). In those days the paint was specially mixed and Robert Wallwork painted the vehicles by hand with a brush! Now operating over 40 trucks, the company is easily identified by its eye-catching green livery.

Below: *Wallwork's vacuum heat treatment department.*

Above: *Pouring metal at Wallwork's Cast Alloys foundry.*

The company expanded with sites in Birmingham (1989) and Cambridge (1997). Owing to the lack of suitable premises in Cambridge, Wallwork purchased a field and contracted Peel Construction from Ramsbottom to build the new factory.

Wallwork purchased another site on the opposite side of Rochdale Road, on Back Derby Street (now Derby Way), in the mid-1990s. The building, which was formerly used by Bury Council and Norweb, is believed to have been originally owned by the Bury Co-operative Brewing and Distilling Co. Ltd (1861) which also owned the Robin Hood public house at that time. It is now used to house Wallwork Cast Alloys, which is the only working foundry remaining in Bury.

Further expansion in 2005 saw Wallwork purchase the ex-Wheeler Tubes site in Hacking Street, which has now become the group head office.

Now employing over 100 people at the Lord Street site and 270 people throughout the country, Wallwork is the second largest heat treatment company in the UK.

Above: *The original entrance to the company's Lord Street works.*

Holy Cross College
Handing on the light

Holy Cross College, formerly known for many years as Bury Convent Grammar School (BCGS), has returned in recent years to the oldest form of its name, as it began as Holy Cross School in 1878.

The college has changed and developed immeasurably since those early days and has become one of the most well-known and celebrated academic institutions in the region. Its reputation is well-known to the people of Bury – and indeed far beyond Bury – and generations of families still ensure their young people have the chance of studying within its hallowed and historic walls.

***Top:** A classroom in 1907.*

***Above:** A School trip to Ashworth Valley in 1883.*

There would never have been a Holy Cross College in Bury, were it not for the Kulturkampf in Germany in the 19th Century. Under the leadership of Bismarck, the German government was pursuing a policy of religious and ethnic prejudice against Catholics, Poles and others at that time. It was much less severe than the Nazi religious and ethnic persecutions that came later, but is said to have influenced them.

This led to a number of religious sisters being forced out of Germany just at the time when Bishop (later Cardinal) Vaughan of the Salford Diocese was searching for teaching sisters to improve educational opportunities for children in his diocese, and not least in Bury. It was an example of how light and resurrection could be brought out of a very dark situation – the way of the Cross.

The first sisters in Bury were led by Sister Iphigénie (Julie Bruckner), a member of the Congregation of the Daughters of the Cross, which had been founded by Blessed Marie Thérèse (Jeanne Haze) in Liège, Belgium in 1833. The order had spread to Germany by 1851. The sisters whom the Bishop invited to Bury were running a school in Dusseldorf until 1878, and the move to England was not an easy transition. At first, they were without even such bare necessities such as chairs, tables, cups and saucers. As Sister Iphigénie later wrote: 'We began on the feast of the Holy Cross... and the Cross has been with us all the way'.

However, from small beginnings, charging pupils a penny a week and receiving wonderful assistance from the people of Bury, the sisters were eventually able to gather together the essentials. The cramped conditions in their first premises in Bank Street necessitated a move to Derby House, further down Manchester Road, and very soon another move further down again to The Ferns, a building which remains a key part of the Summerfield Building in the present college. Early work was in the parish school of St Marie's, as well as in St Marie's Church, and there are strong links with the parish church to this day.

Education for all was a relatively new idea in those days and, as the sisters expanded their school and its premises, they expanded their work to include the training of teachers. As these trainees came from other parts of the country and from Ireland, they

***Above:** The school art room in 1935. **Right:** The original college chapel. **Below Right:** The college chapel today.*

needed a place to live, so the need for accommodation grew, and the concept of a boarding school evolved. Gradually, the convent school expanded and new buildings were added to the houses originally purchased with, in 1887, the foundation stone of the purpose built Holy Cross School being laid in the Golden Jubilee of Queen Victoria's reign.

Sister Iphigénie (after whom the modern, second-floor sports hall is named) eventually progressed to be Provincial of the Congregation of the Daughters of the Cross in London. As the new century dawned, after the hard work of several more pioneering sisters, the school continued to flourish under Sister Willibalda (Christine Kanovenberg), who held office as Head from 1901–1918. In 1905, it ceased to be a public elementary school and began work as a secondary school. The preparatory school for the younger pupils then functioned separately. This was the origin of Bury Catholic Preparatory School which continues to this day. The secondary school was entitled to grants from the Board of Education.

Money was obtained from various other sources and buildings erected about that time that are still in use – including the 'Tower', which is part of the corner of the site originally named after Our Lady of Grace. In 1910, however, a great fire damaged the boarding school at the top and back of Summerfield, adjacent to The Ferns. Records state that the rebuilding and refurbishment costs were £500. By this time the school had begun to be called Bury Convent and under that name many illustrious former students were educated.

One of the fondly remembered features of the early buildings was the simple but beautiful chapel, which was built to echo the appearance of the Mother House chapel in rue Hors-Château, Liège, Belgium, where - at the time of writing - the body of Blessed Marie Thérèse rests. In 2017 her remains will be enshrined in Liège Cathedral. Problems with inadequate foundations in the Chapel at Bury led, however, to its eventual demolition - after a period hosting the college's drama students. A wonderful new chapel now forms part of the newest building, Kentigern, named after Sister Mary Kentigern (Margaret Kirk), who was Head from 1918–1931 and also went on to lead the Daughters of the Cross nationally as Provincial. The new chapel still contains the altar from the original chapel, before which so many girls were confirmed or took First Holy Communion, slightly remodeled to create an Altar, Ambo (lectern) and Chair for the celebrating Priest.

The sixth form work started in 1920, followed by the purchase of the large house known as Agincourt in 1922 and the playing fields next door soon after. Agincourt has since been demolished, making way for the Blessed Marie Thérèse building opened at Christmas, 2004.

Above: The Emilie Mary Building pictured in 1952.

Readers who attended the school in the 1930s may recall the tumult of 'the year of three kings' – 1936. It began with pupils mourning the death of King George V, then celebrating the proclamation of King Edward VIII, then trying to make sense of the latter's abdication and marriage to Mrs Simpson, and eventually celebrating the Coronation of King George VI and Queen Elizabeth (later known as the Queen Mother) not long after. If the abdication crisis was not enough to puzzle young minds what of war, with all its scares, tribulations and deprivations?

Fortunately, the school had an exceptional leader in those dark days. In 1929 a new sister had arrived to join the teaching staff – diminutive in size but big in heart - who taught Latin and English with enthusiasm but - equally enthusiastically - led rambles over Holcombe Hill and elsewhere. She was full of fun, and yet earned great respect from her students, who felt she was always understanding of their worries and concerns. This was Sister Emilie Mary (Frances Murray), who was to serve as Head from 1939-1966. She came into office as the Second World War started. Under her leadership in 1944 Holy Cross became a Direct Grant School, known as Bury Convent Grammar School. When the war ended in 1945 numbers began to increase.

Below: An original doorway with stone carvings at Holy Cross College.

The boarding school closed in 1950 to make room for the rapidly expanding day school. The long-awaited building programme swung into action and has not ceased since. The Emilie Mary building erected in the 1950s (and named after Sister) is still in use today, albeit with a new roof, new windows and new, attractive cladding fitted in 2011. Paradoxically, it looks like a building of the 21st century, whereas some of our buildings which are, have a pleasingly traditional look, with brick, stained glass and stone. Modern students often cite the beautiful architecture of the college - not least the Victorian buildings with their exquisite stone carvings - as a factor in their choice of the college.

The sixth form that started with single figures in the early 1920s grew to between two and three hundred. The school roll shot up to over seven hundred. As growth continued, further major changes were soon on the horizon. In the late 1970s the Government decided to end the direct grant which funded poorer pupils to attend the most outstanding schools in the country.

Three choices were available - the school could close, it could go 'independent' or, thirdly, join forces with the local authority as part of a planned reorganization into a 'tertiary' system, with most schools becoming 11-16, alongside a Further Education College and a Sixth Form College for post-16 students. The school authorities chose the latter option and the school became a Catholic, co-educational sixth form college for the whole community, welcoming students from all backgrounds alongside the original students. With young men joining the young women for the first time, it was felt that BCGS, with its echoes of 'Convent' life, needed to revert to the original name of Holy Cross!

***Above:** School leavers in 1973.*

In its early years as a Sixth Form College, Holy Cross often struggled for funding, as this was historically based. The well-off local authorities did well, but Bury had to wait for 'convergence', which took a while to arrive. Without the generosity of the Daughters of the Cross at this point, not least in funding a major building programme, the college's progress would not have been so dramatic.

Happily, things improved over time with Government grants, continued help from the Daughters, and the students' own fund raising efforts as well as excellent financial management and stewardship. Eventually the college developed a full range of well-deserved state-of-the-art facilities which combined traditional appearance with the latest in technology.

The greatest resource a school or college can have is passionate, brilliant and committed staff, however. Holy Cross has always been fortunate to have many wonderful heads, teachers, support staff, governors and principals serving the school and college over the years. They have enriched the lives of scores of pupils and students and staff and made Bury a better place by their presence and effort. The religious significance of their lives of service has added to the growth in spirituality of hundreds of people.

HOLY CROSS COLLEGE

An education at Holy Cross is always about much more than the excellent exam results for which it is famous. It is about developing leadership skills, humanity, compassion, a set of values and a sense of service, an ability to study and work independently but also in a team. These values are priceless, indeed divine, and the college welcomes all Christians, those of other faiths, and indeed all people of goodwill to grow in understanding of them and of the things that give life meaning and make it worthwhile.

In all its successes the school and college have held on firmly to these truths and the beauty of their two mottos: *Omnis scientia vera est a Deo* - All true knowledge comes from God - and *In hoc signo vinces* - In this sign you will conquer. The latter, of course, is a reference to the sign and way of the Cross, and reflects the great vision of Constantine in 312 AD which seemed to repeat itself in a certain way at the foundation of the Daughters of the Cross. To this day,

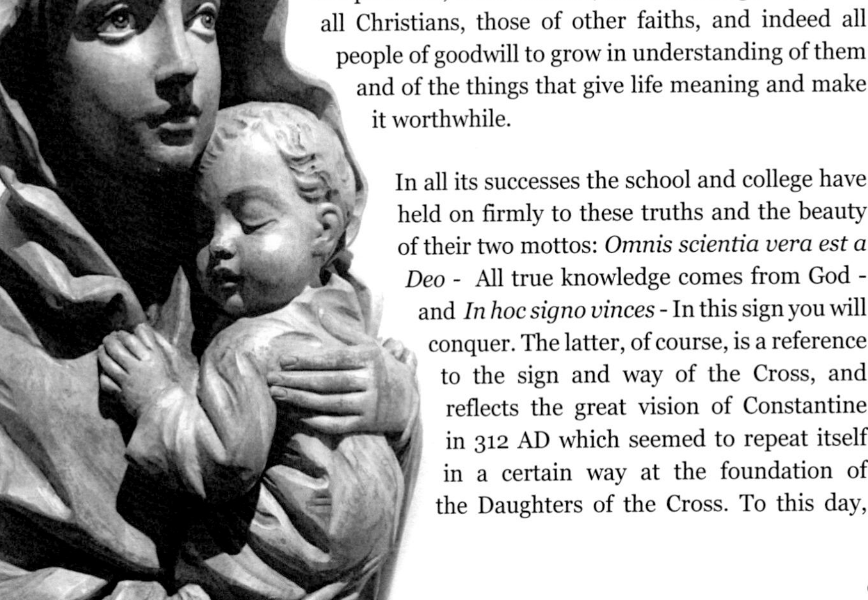

***Right:** Statue of Our Lady from the present Chapel.*

Above: *University Centre students graduating.*

the cross, with the corona or halo of light seen by Blessed Marie Thérèse in her founding vision, remains our badge.

The college has an excellent reputation for music, drama, art and other creative disciplines as well as sciences, social sciences, humanities and arts in general. It also has a great reputation - and huge success - in sport. How can this be when there are no playing fields to be seen when you approach the site? In fact, the college uses many excellent playing fields nearby, although, as mentioned, it has wonderful sports hall on site.

In the early days it did have a small playing field and tennis courts, but these eventually made way for yet another new building, named after Sister Mary Aidan (Mary Kelly) which opened in 2001. Sister Mary was Head (twice, from 1966-1976 and from 1985-1994) and also, like a number of her great predecessors, served as Provincial of the Daughters of the Cross in this country (twice, from 1976-1985 and from 1994-2003). She was greatly loved and is still spoken of very fondly by old girls of Bury Convent Grammar School and former students of Holy Cross College. Until shortly before she died in 2008 she was still active in the college she loved, in the Chaplaincy and on the Governing Body.

Below: *A Level students celebrating on results day.*

There was a time when 700 students aged 11-18 seemed to be the maximum for the campus. Today there are approximately 2,000 students aged 16-19. But that is not all - there are many people in our area who, for one reason or another, left formal education early but who would now like to return to it. Holy Cross has the facilities to help them do so. In conjunction, initially, with Liverpool Hope University, Holy Cross decided to use its evenings to provide degree, diploma or other forms of extended education. That initiative flourished and now more than 600 local people are taking advantage of the courses every year. The core partnership with Hope has extended to Edge Hill University, St Mary's University and Newman University. Holy Cross University Centre offers full honours degrees entirely taught in Bury, and 'top ups' for those who have foundation degrees. Despite a later start in many cases, and less conventional routes into higher education, our students gain an exceptionally high number of first class and 2:1 degrees.

The sixth form side of the college also now rejoices in the fact that it has been placed amongst the top sixth form colleges in the country, is a member of the 'Maple Group' and has been awarded Beacon Status. It is regularly in the top ten nationally for results, especially for A* and A grades, and was recently second in the country for success rates. Many former students have gone on to Oxford, Cambridge and other excellent universities, as well as making names for themselves around the world in interesting careers.

None of the developments which have taken place down the years could have happened without the courage and bravery of those first Sisters who arrived in Bury with Sister Iphigénie in 1878. In the fullness of time those sisters' places were taken by devoted successors who have appreciated the mission of the founders and built on the spiritual ethos they passed down.

That mission and ethos is still palpable today. It is perhaps the greatest reason why students and staff feel so happy here and why Holy Cross is such a strong community, attracting students and staff from far and wide. Whatever the future may hold, today's staff are well aware that they are the custodians of a precious inheritance and their task is to keep that torch alight and, in their turn too, to pass it on.

Below: *The new Kentigern building, blending tradition with innovation.*

William Hare Group
Engineering steel for iconic projects

Steel fabricated in Bury has been used in some of the UK's most iconic projects and has been shipped across the globe to form the backbone of an ever-lengthening list of prestigious schemes.

The William Hare Group is primarily involved in the production and erection of structural steelwork to a variety of markets in both the UK and the United Arab Emirates as well as shipping fabricated steel to projects around the world.

Among the portfolio of high profile projects are some of the best-known structures in the North West including the Trafford Centre and Manchester Arena, Manchester Airport and Liverpool John Lennon Airport, the Lowry, and Media City in Salford Quays.

Further afield, William Hare has completed a number of projects in London, including the Olympic Stadium Roof Conversion and 20 Fenchurch St, commonly known as the Walkie Talkie. Projects in the UAE include; the Mall of the Emirates in Dubai and Al Dar HQ and ADIC Towers, both in Abu Dhabi.

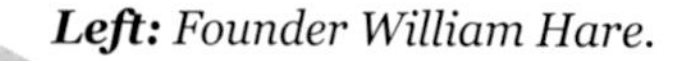

***Left:** Founder William Hare.*

The William Hare Group head office is located in Bury and the Group operates facilities in Bury, Scarborough, Wigan, Wetherby, and Grantham and has an office in London. Overseas, the Group has manufacturing facilities in Abu Dhabi and Dubai with offices in India, Singapore, Korea and the Philippines.

It is not overstating the case to say that the business has come an incredibly long way since being founded as erection engineers by William Hare in Bolton in 1888. The company predominantly concentrated on the building and dismantling of structures and mechanical plant items.

Erecting large cast iron/steel items was a specialist service so workshops were highly dependent on companies like William Hare.

In 1925, William Hare Jr took over the reins of the company and continued to operate the business from his home in Bolton. By this time the company was erecting the majority of steel frame buildings in the Bolton and Manchester area. The most prestigious of these was the Bolton Town Hall Crescent building constructed between 1931 and 1939 . This huge scheme provided welcome employment to many families during the economic hardship that north England faced throughout the 1930s.

In 1945, after his return from the Second World War, Bartle Hodgkiss, son-in-law of William Hare Jr, joined the board of directors. William Hare, his daughter, Joan, and Bartle Hodgkiss incorporated William Hare Ltd in 1946.

***Left:** Town Hall Crescent Building, Bolton.*

***Above:** Weston Street.* ***Below:** An artist's impression of the Acresfield office in 1950.*

The company made a strategic decision to enter the steel fabrication market to capitalise on the post war construction boom. William Hare Jr was primarily responsible for the erection side of the business, Bartle Hodgkiss for engineering and fabrication.

An office was opened up at Lloyds Bank Chambers, Howell Croft, Bolton and the fabrication of steelwork was carried out at the Hatfield and Bridgeman street yards. The company began to expand beyond the North West and started to carry out projects throughout the United Kingdom.

In 1950, offices moved to Acresfield, Bolton and this became the company's first registered office. A lease was then taken out on the site of the dismantled Wellington Mill in Weston Street, Bolton. William Hare began erection and fabrication from the facility and opened an office there as well. Up until this time, the erection element of the business was still the main focus, however in 1952; the company became a fully operational structural engineering company, offering full service from greenfield projects to the refurbishment of buildings and plants.

In 1960, William Hare Jr sadly passed away aged 55 while on holiday in Falmouth. Bartle Hodgkiss then took over the reins of the company. By this time William Hare had broken into the petrochemical market, carrying out a number of projects on behalf of Shell, Woodall Duckham and others.

In the 1970's, the son and daughter of Bartle and Joan Hodgkiss - David and Susan - started work with the company, gaining experience throughout all departments of the business.

In 1977 William Hare Ltd won the prestigious Queen's Award for Export. The award was formally presented to Bartle Hodgkiss at a special ceremony by the Mayor of Bolton, the Mayor of Tyldesley and the Lord Lieutenant of Lancashire.

Later that year, the California Engineering Company Limited which had been established in Bury since the early 1960's was bought by William Hare. At the time of the purchase, the facility had one complete bay, a partly completed extension and internal offices. Between 1977 and 1990, William Hare completed the extension and added an additional six bays. This was a significant investment to the facility and increased the size of the site from 8,500m^2 to 25,000m^2. In the late 1990's the company invested in two more production facilities based in Scarborough and Wetherby.

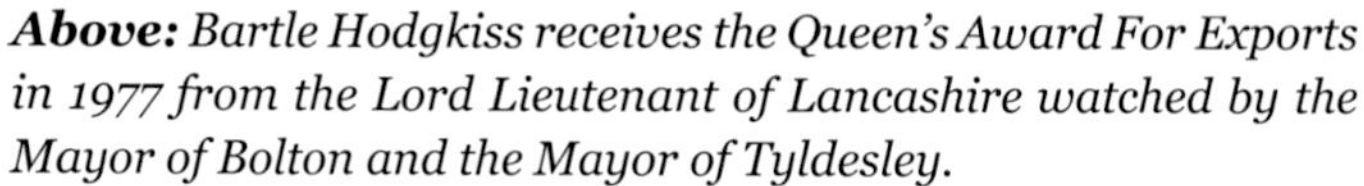

Above: *Bartle Hodgkiss receives the Queen's Award For Exports in 1977 from the Lord Lieutenant of Lancashire watched by the Mayor of Bolton and the Mayor of Tyldesley.*

Before the turn of the Millennium, William Hare Group Ltd was established, the business was restructured and David Hodgkiss was appointed Chief Executive Officer. In 2000, the Group's Head Office was moved to Brandlesholme House in Bury, staff from both Bury and Weston Street sites were united under the one roof for the first time. The business cut its ties to Bolton and firmly established itself as a Bury business. By the mid-2000s, the company's production accounted for over 50 per cent of all UK fabricated steel exported internationally.

Throughout the millennium the business continued to expand dramatically. The Group opened an engineering office in Chennai, India and purchased two further steel fabrication facilities in the UAE as well as expanding operations in South East Asia.

In 2009, Susan Hodgkiss was awarded a CBE for her services to industry and for her significant contribution to the community and charitable organisations.

By 2011, William Hare Group became the first UK steel manufacture to be awarded the EC Certificate of Factory Control Production (CE Marking). A year later, William Hare's UAE operations also achieved CE Marking, becoming the first steel fabrication facility in the region to do so.

In 2013, the Chairman, Bartle Hodgkiss passed away aged 94, Susan Hodgkiss then took over as the Group Chair. During his time, the Chairman had transformed the business from a small local erection company and laid the foundations for the global structural steel engineering company that exists today.

Left: *Bury Facility (California Works in 1977).*

Left and above: *Brandlesholme House, the group's head office in Bury, pictured in the 1920s and in the present day.*

The History of Brandlesholme House

Brandlesholme House was completed in 1897 but was built on the site of the Old Brandlesholme Hall, which dates back to the 14th century. For upwards of four centuries this was the residence of the Greenhalgh family who owned not only the lands around the house but other estates elsewhere in Lancashire. It is claimed that Charles Dickens even stayed at the house in 1838 and that he wrote the early chapters of the book 'Nicholas Nickleby' as he sat by the fountain.

In the 1870s the owners decided to replace the ancient buildings by building a larger house more suitable to their status as landowners and industrialists. For the next 60 years the house was associated with either paper-making or textiles until 1944 when the Corporation of Bury converted it to a residential hostel. In 1977 it was converted into offices by Holden Consultants.

The house has had three main extensions since it was taken over as an office. William Hare Group took on the building in the year 2000, modernised, restored and transformed it into a building befitting of a global headquarters.

In June, 2014, CEO David Hodgkiss was awarded an OBE for services to manufacturing and exporting.

In 2015, William Hare expanded again with the acquisition of a local fabrication company based in Wigan. The move secured the jobs of some 60 skilled workers as well as increasing the production capacity of fabricated steel.

The same year, the company donated steel and engineering expertise to the East Lancashire Railway's Bolton Street Station in Bury, the donation was used to complete the platform 1 canopy.

Today the William Hare Group is the largest privately owned structural steelwork contractor in Europe, and has

Right: *A large delivery in Bolton.*

Above: *Chancellor George Osborne and Bury MP David Nuttall are shown some of the latest fabrication technology at the Bury Facility by Phil Molyneux, of the William Hare Group* ***Below:*** *Bury Facility interior.*

worked in over 50 countries on some of the world's most innovative and sustainable construction projects.

The group has a turnover of £200 million, a worldwide capacity of 165,000 tonnes per annum and employs over 2,000 staff.

The William Hare Bury Facility employs more than 100 skilled workers, while the Group Head Office at Brandlesholme houses more than 200 staff. This makes the William Hare Group one of the largest employers in the Bury area.

Brandlesholme House and the Bury Facility have hosted a variety of overseas clients and foreign ministers. In 2015, Chancellor of the Exchequer, George Osborne MP, visited the Bury Facility to promote his vision of the Northern Powerhouse. He was given a guided tour, met apprentices and got hands-on with some of the latest fabrication techniques.

The Group and its employees play their part in supporting local charities. William Hare backs local business and has sponsored categories in the Made in Bury Business Awards while employees

Above: *Exterior of the Bury Facility*

have given up their time, donated their money and continue to go out of their way to support the local community.

Above: *Aldar HQ, Abu Dhabi.*

Above: *Chill Factore, Manchester.*

Above: *Olympic Stadium, London.*

Milliken Industrials Ltd

Unique product is a life-saver

STRETCHED across the North Atlantic Ocean, 12 million linear metres of high quality fabric produced each year in Bury would roll out to South Carolina, USA – and most of the way back again.

Not that anyone is going to put that to the test but it does at least give an indication of the volume of airbag material produced by Milliken Industrials Ltd from its historic Wellington Mill premises situated a stone's throw from the River Irwell.

Why South Carolina? That's where you will find the headquarters of Milliken and Company, a leading international textile and chemicals firm with more than 7,000 employees and 39 manufacturing sites worldwide, making it one of the world's largest privately owned companies.

The specialist cloth produced in Bury for Milliken European Airbag Products is used by most big motor manufacturers, among them Mercedes, BMW and Audi but, as the plant's vice-president, Graham Swann says, it is a product that, hopefully, no-one gets to see!

Both Milliken and Wellington Mill have proud histories which run almost parallel. Built in the Lancashire heartlands of the industrial revolution in 1864, Wellington Mill has always been a manufacturer of textile products, specialising initially in heavy cotton fabrics, mainly canvases and tyre cords.

Left: *Roger Milliken*

Milliken dates back to 1865 when Seth Milliken and William Deering founded the Deering Milliken Company, a small woollen fabrics company in Portland, Maine, USA. Three years later Deering left to start his own company and Seth Milliken moved the company headquarters to New York City, the centre of the American textile industry around that time.

The company invested in a new plant in Pacolet, South Carolina, in 1884 and from relatively humble beginnings the manufacturing operation grew rapidly. Roger Milliken assumed the presidency of the company in 1947 upon the death of his father, Gerrish Milliken. He remained chief executive officer until 2006 and served as chairman of the board right up to his death in December, 2010.

Milliken bought its first European operation in 1964 when it purchased the Wellington Mill plant. Two important landmarks were reached in 2014 – the 150th anniversary of the opening of the mill and 50 years under the wing of Milliken and Company.

At the time of the purchase the Wellington plant produced cotton ducting but was soon converted to synthetic fibres and branched out into new market areas supplying products to the automotive industry.

Left: *Wellington Mill in the 1950s.*

In 1994 the plant invested in new weaving and scouring equipment to allow production of airbag fabric which also required significant expansion of the plant. Success in this market led to further growth in 2005 to accommodate new sizing, beaming, weaving, scouring and coating equipment. To provide greater value to its customers the plant has added laser cutting to its list of production equipment.

The heavy industrial production was moved to Milliken's sister plant in Gent, Belgium, allowing Wellington Mill to go to full production of airbags. The number of weaving machines increased meaning that in 2015 around 37,000 metres a day were produced of high quality closely woven fabric going into automotive airbags worldwide.

A wide range is currently in production in coated and uncoated nylon and polyester which go into front, side and knee bags and also into side curtains. The business also supplies cut parts to automotive seating

Above: *Graham Swann.* ***Below:*** *The current weave room. More than 140 people are employed by Milliken in Bury.*

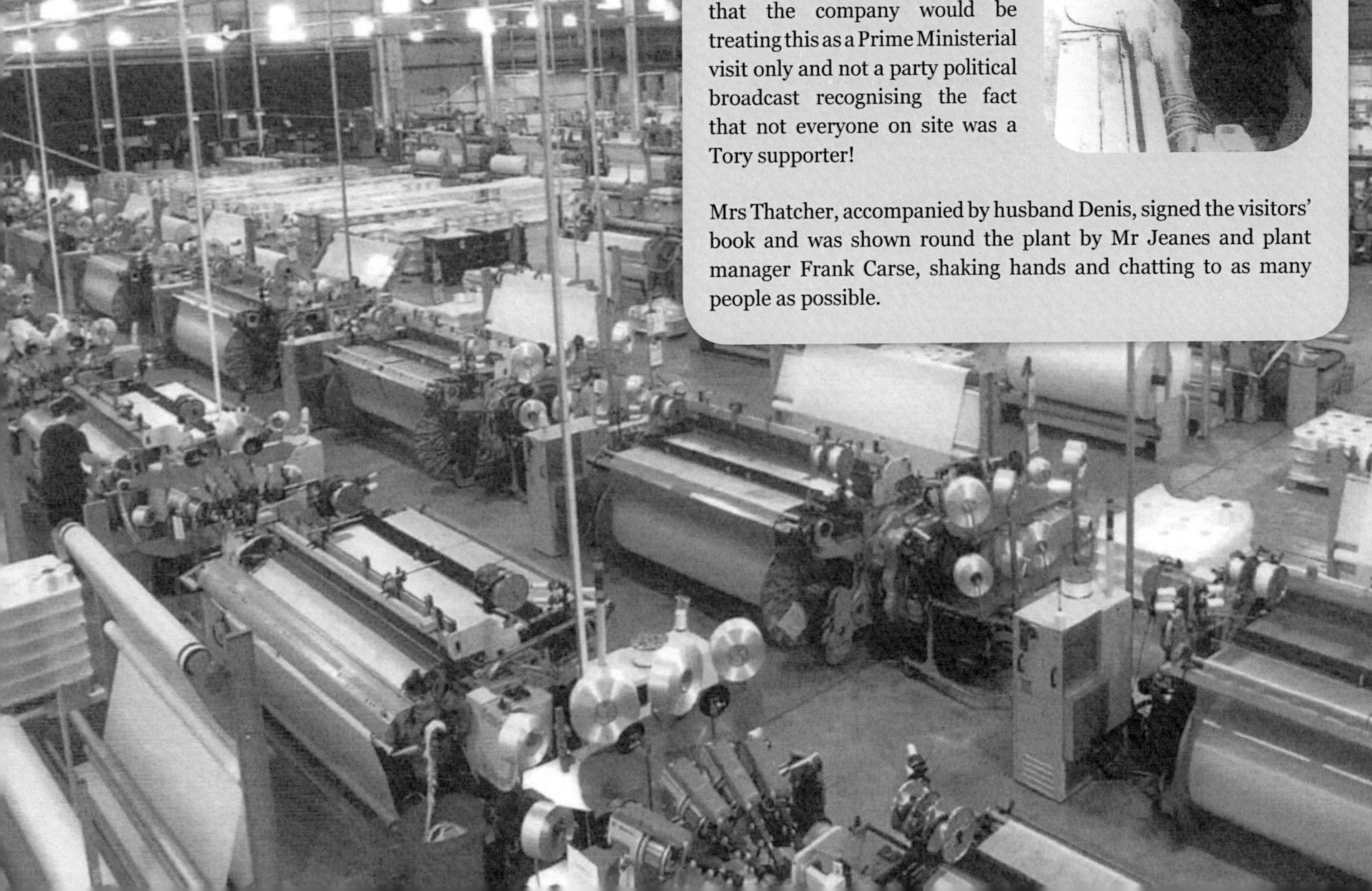

PM's happy memories

Former Prime Minister Margaret Thatcher took away happy memories of a visit to Milliken Industrials Ltd during the 1987 General Election campaign.

For not only did she enjoy a guided tour of this fascinating business she subsequently saw her candidate for Bury North, Alistair Burt MP, romp to a comfortable victory.

Managing director Clive Jeanes pointed out to Milliken employees that the company would be treating this as a Prime Ministerial visit only and not a party political broadcast recognising the fact that not everyone on site was a Tory supporter!

Mrs Thatcher, accompanied by husband Denis, signed the visitors' book and was shown round the plant by Mr Jeanes and plant manager Frank Carse, shaking hands and chatting to as many people as possible.

Top: *Workers at the Waterside Mill Company in the 1950s.* ***Above:*** *A group of employees in the weave room.*

companies for use in airbag chutes allowing the side bags located in the side of the seat to deploy smoothly.

They are products that have made Milliken a global success – and the source of envy for other manufacturers struggling to increase their productivity. The Wellington factory is one of only a few to have survived industrial decline in the region and has become a model for high value manufacturing within its American private company. Colleagues visit from Milliken's textile and chemical plants across the globe to learn how this fabric maker consistently beats productivity targets.

Besides the technological advances, Milliken European Airbag Products has implemented into its processes the way that the company and its employees work on a day-to-day basis both with machinery and with each other, catapulting the organisation to new production heights.

Over the last two years Milliken has competed for a number of awards with the aim of testing itself externally against the best businesses in the UK and to drive forward its continuous improvement programme

The company's achievements have been acknowledged by their peers, culminating in a string of industry awards. Probably the highest prized of these was the 'World Class Manufacturing' honour awarded to Milliken at the Manufacturer of the Year awards held in Birmingham in November, 2013. The honour is generally regarded by those in the know as the prize most worth winning.

In addition, the company won the UK 2013 Best Factory Award in the Household and General Products category and in the same year they received the Outstanding Achievement honour in the 'Made In Bury' awards. In 2014 the company received the UK Fashion and Textile Association 'Let's Make It Here' award.

This is how the Bury Times reported the successful takeover of Waterside Mill Co in 1964

A £540,000 take-over bid by one of the largest textile firms in the United States for the Waterside Mill Co (Bury) has succeeded and declared unconditional.

The offer, by Deering Milliken Inc of New York, of two shillings for each of Waterside's 5,400,000 ordinary one shilling shares has been accepted by more that 90 per cent of the shareholders.

The American firm intends in due course to acquire compulsorily any outstanding shares but, meanwhile, the offer remains open for acceptance.

Mr T.F. Buxton, chairman of Waterside, and Mr J.E. Williams will retire from the board and will receive payments of £5,000 and £1,000 respectively for loss of office.

A private company, Deering Milliken is one of the largest textile companies in the United States and its operations cover a large range of textiles manufactured from wool, cotton and man-made fibres.

Increasing emphasis has been placed in recent years by the firm on industrial fabrics and it is intended that Waterside shall become the base for operations in this field in the European Free Trade Area.

The Waterside Mill Co (Bury) was formed in 1886 and their Wellington Mill was acquired in 1929. Principal products are tyre cord, canvas and a variety of fabrics for industrial use.

More than 300 people are employed at the two mills.

Above: *The current creeling frame prior to sizing.* ***Top right:*** *Trimmed up for the Coronation of Queen Elizabeth 11.* ***Below:*** *A bird's eye view of Wellington Mill in the early 1960s.*

The awards come as just reward for a company that prides itself on team effort. Says Graham Swann: "It has been the investment, engagement and trust in our workforce that has enabled our business at Wellington Mill to truly flourish."

Charities benefit from feel-good factor

There's a feel-good factor about Milliken that stems from its desire to help others.

One beneficiary has been Bury Cancer Support Centre which has received cash and furnishings for its base in Bolton Road, Bury.

Centre manager Jan Katana is full of praise for the company's backing. "For the past four years we have been Milliken's charity of the year and we are exceptionally grateful to them for their continuing support and the recognition of what we do."

Mrs Katana singled out for special praise Bury-based employee Janet Hutchinson who co-ordinates the company's fundraising initiatives for the cancer support centre.

"The centre costs £10,000 a month to run and the efforts of Janet and her team are very much appreciated."

Dunsters Farm
The cream of the crop

Bury has been home to Dunsters Farm for over 50 years. Starting out as a milk round, the business has developed to become the foodservice it is today, delivering chilled and ambient food and drink to customers throughout the North of England.

The third generation family business has seen many changes since those early days with the late Les Ratcliffe, MBE, and his wife, Nancy, working tirelessly to build the business despite many challenges along the way.

Les bought a milk round from his father, James, in 1954 paying the full market price. The round covered Ramsbottom, Holcombe Brook and Greenmount. He went on to buy a few smaller rounds and combined them to extend coverage to Brandlesholme and Elton.

Above: *A painting of the original Dunsters Farm circa 1954.*

Four years later Les and Nancy moved to Dunsters Farm, a run down piggery in Brandlesholme, with daughter Elizabeth who was one at the time. They had two milk lads - George Ormston and Terry Jackson - who helped with the rounds.

At Dunsters Farm, the family sold free range hens and Elizabeth - now one of the directors remembers having day old chicks in the bedroom. At Christmas, the whole family helped out to pluck the hens ready for delivery to customers. Deliveries started in the family's Morris Minor van until they invested in an electric milk float. Although advanced for its time, it was very slow but ended up being the family transport for many years!

Soon after moving the family to Brandlesholme, Les met Edgar Dickinson (of Longley Farm) who asked Les if he would start selling cream on the milk rounds. Les also supplied local shops. Clifford Howard, an old school friend who had worked on Bury market and at Ross Frozen Foods, started work as a salesman around this time.

Les met a Dutchman in Clitheroe who was making something new called yogurt. None of Les's customers had heard of yogurt and selling it was hard as many regarded it as 'sour milk'. Les, however, was convinced there was potential and offered the yogurt on sale or return. The mixed reaction from customers was not helped when some of the yogurts started exploding! Nevertheless, Les persevered and eventually moved yogurt production to Elm Farm in Oxfordshire and later persuaded Edgar Dickinson at Longley Farm in Holmfirth to make it. Ironically, Dunsters Farm

Left: *The Ratcliffe Family, Nancy, Hilary, Heather, Sally, Elizabeth, Les.*

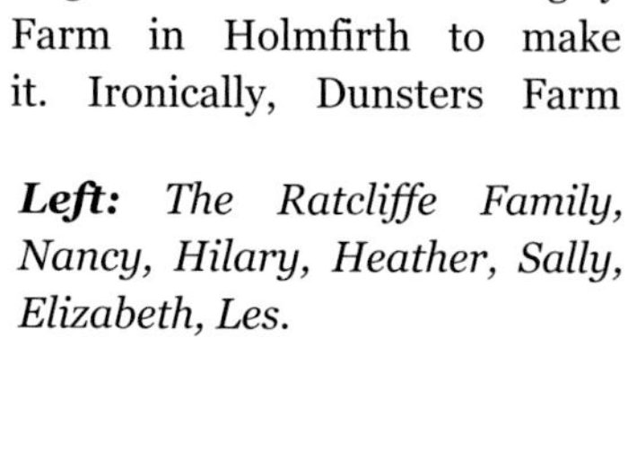

Above: *Dunsters Farm circa 1984.*

yogurts are now made back in Clitheroe - though exploding pots are a thing of the past!

Over the years, the product list grew, with cottage cheese, coleslaw, lemon cheese and pickles being added along with tinned tongue and ham and gallons of cream being delivered every day to the confectionery trade, greengrocers, butchers and other independent stores in the local area.

Growth meant that more vehicles were required. At that time, they were insulated, not refrigerated like today's fleet. These insulated vehicles were very unusual for their time but allowed the growing Dunsters Farm team to expand their coverage. Firstly, it moved north of Bury and started selling in towns such as Bacup but this proved much harder than home turf. When Syd Cartwright joined the team, attention shifted to South Manchester, an area which grew quickly and in 1961 Les opened a unit on the old Smithfield Market in Manchester. Dunsters became a limited company in 1963.

Right: *The Model T Ford at a trade show.*

During the 1960s Dunsters worked with Tom Wilkinson from Unigate Dairies to establish a range of own label cheese. Unlike today's pre-packed blocks, these were bought in large 40lb blocks and brought back to Dunsters Farm to be cut and vacuum packed by long-serving member of staff Lillian Lucas. It was also during this time that Dunsters further expanded its own label range to include cream and cottage cheese.

Following the success of the Manchester Market unit, Dunsters opened up a unit at Liverpool wholesale fruit and vegetable market which meant more early mornings for the family but it quickly grew and eventually two vans delivered from Liverpool market to customers around Liverpool and Southport.

Business continued to grow throughout the 70s but not without many challenges and obstacles along the way. Elizabeth recalls one particular Christmas when there was a national milk shortage and Dickinson's only had enough for their own supply. With customers desperate for cream, Les set off to scour the country to get hold of tankers of milk that could be delivered to Dickinson's so that Dunsters production could commence. However, with Christmas rapidly approaching, Nancy and daughters Heather and Hilary had to go and help make it while Elizabeth stayed home at Dunsters Farm to deal with the many phone calls from customers demanding their cream for Christmas.

Left: *Jeremy at an exhibition circa 1990.*

In late 1979, Jeremy Mathew - the current MD - Elizabeth, one of her sisters, Heather, and long serving staff member, Jack Rothwell, went to Birmingham to establish Dunsters Farm on the wholesale market. This was a new area for the business so after the early morning shift on the market, the four of them went out canvassing for new business in the afternoons. The following year Jeremy and Elizabeth got married and moved back from Birmingham for Jeremy to take on the role of General Manager.

During the 1980s, the business moved to a bigger unit at Manchester Market and operated as a cash and carry. It was around this time that Les became Chairman - a move that saw Jeremy become Managing Director, a role he holds to this day. Les continued to play an active part in the business despite his enthusiastic involvement in local charities, becoming the first President of the East Lancashire Railway and Chairman of Bury Hospice. His tireless commitment to charity work earned him an MBE in 2000, an honour of which he was immensely proud. His citation and medal are displayed at the depot today.

Left: *Van sales price list from 1994.*

The 1980s saw the rise in popularity of salads in the UK and Dunsters worked with Geest to produce own label coleslaw and salads to meet this demand. During this period, sales soared and Dunsters Farm became Geest's second largest customer after Marks and Spencer!

Another significant milestone was the advent of cooked meats. Terry Nortley joined Dunsters Farm from George Little's in Manchester and had a background in cooked meats - something Dunsters had never previously sold - Jeremy and Terry jumped on a plane to Ireland to secure a beef and turkey supplier. This was a big step forward for the company and although cooked meats are now sourced in England, they continue to be a big seller.

Les's son, James, joined the business after leaving school at a time of significant change for the business. After years of handwritten notes, Dunsters purchased its first computer which was the size of a large washing machine! It was also during this time in the late 80s that the business opened up depots in Kirkham and Yorkshire and the world of yogurt changed forever with the advent of Muller's revolutionary split pot – something no one ever thought would catch on! Dunsters also continued to launch line after line of own label products from fruit juice to margarine, butter to spray cream.

In 1991 the firm moved from the original Dunsters Farm in Brandlesholme to a new home in Tottington. This was also around the time that the business moved from van sales to telesales. This was a fundamental change in the business model that allowed for greater growth.

During the 1990s the business won a significant contract with Sayers the Bakers delivering to around 70 bakery shops in and

Above: *The 1 millionth pack of Dunsters Fruit Juice - 1988.*

around Liverpool until the closure of that side of their business.

John Clarke joined the business at the age of 59 and his enthusiasm and experience were instrumental in securing the Booth's contract, something which ensured further growth for the business. John remained with the business until he retired aged 67 and Booth's moved to their own distribution.

In 2006 Dunsters moved to a purpose-built depot at Waterfold Park, Bury, which enabled the rapid growth of ambient lines, in particular an expansion in fruit juices, water and milk-based drinks. This expansion of the product portfolio allowed the business to move into the schools market. Today, Dunsters' drivers deliver to schools and colleges throughout the North of England and North Wales.

In 2014, James decided to leave the business to pursue other business interests and the third generation of the family, Hannah and Tom (Jeremy and Elizabeth's children) joined the firm. The company is now looking forward to the future growth and opportunities as it heads towards its sixth decade.

As with any small family business, Dunsters Farm has had to constantly adapt and change in order to secure its future. It still sells cheese, cooked meats, coleslaw and, of course, yogurts but the business looks rather different today. Despite all the changes and challenges over the years, Dunsters has remained true to its Bury roots.

After all these years, Dunsters still goes to Manchester market five days a week and continues to serve independent shops and businesses in and around Bury. Its trucks now reach Cumbria, most of Yorkshire and into North Wales. The customer base may have expanded but its excellent staff of 40 still adhere to Les Ratcliffe's original values of quality food and fair prices - "for people who prefer the best".

Below: *Waterfold Park showing James on the forklift and Transport Manager Geoff Pepper on the truck.*

Albany International

Making the going smoother

Albany International Ltd and the business it took over, James Kenyon and Son, each have long and proud histories and a great deal in common even though they were established more than 3,000 miles apart.

James Kenyon's was founded in Bury in 1664 as a manufacturer of woollen, linen and cotton cloths for machinery. There was a long line of Kenyon's to keep the business going – one of them an MP for the town for eight years.

He is described in the archives as 'a prosperous woollen manufacturer', but it was James Kenyon MP's reputation as a fair employer that won over the electorate.

He was voted in at the 1895 general election as MP for the borough of Bury having stood unsuccessfully in neighbouring Heywood in 1885. He was re-elected in 1900 but resigned his seat in the Commons two years later when he became Steward of the manor of Northstead in 1902. A former Justice of the Peace, James's home was Walshaw Hall, Bury, which later became a residential care home.

Telegrams "KENYON" BURY

"THE JAVELIN"

Telephone Nº 872 BURY

Bought of

JAMES KENYON & SON LIMITED.

Manufacturers of all kinds of Woollen, Linen & Cotton Cloths for Machinery

Your Order Nº

Derby Street Mills,

BURY June 30th 1939

Miss A. Bannister

Above: *Derby Street and Earl Street Mills.* ***Left:*** *An order form for James Kenyon.*

His company had a number of mills in the area – Derby Street Mills, Earl Street, Roach Bank, Pilsworth, Glen, Woolfold and Crimble.

The mill at Derby Street closed in 1971 and became the site of a new shopping and leisure development, The Rock. It was during work on the foundations that archaeology experts unearthed remains of the old mill which was built in 1867 as an addition to Kenyon's expanding empire. Few plans of the mill exist and little is known about its internal layout. Excavation work exposed extensive remains of the steam-driven power plant, including the engine foundations, boiler house and chimney.

Experts said at the time that the finds should not halt development as they did not warrant a preservation order but the remains were drawn, photographed and documented and placed in Bury's archives.

Reports in the Bury Times of the discovery of sections of the mill brought back memories for a former managing director, Ray Shipley, who started as a junior office boy in September, 1949, at the age of 15.

He said that in the early days much of his time was spent traipsing around the sprawling mill looking for the works manager or other senior members of staff who were summoned to meet Kenyon family members in their private offices or to see the various

Left: *The Pilsworth site in April 1970 before construction began.*

salesmen who supplied many of the mill's product requirements.

This meant that he would visit all parts of the mill on a regular basis. "Life in the woollen mill was tough but we had some happy times," said the former boss who retired in 1995 after 46 years service with James Kenyon and Albany.

Meanwhile, Albany International was expanding rapidly - 3,000 miles away across the North Atlantic, The textiles and materials processing company which was founded in 1895 and has its headquarters in Rochester, New Hampshire, USA, operates 19 plants in 10 countries and employs 4,000 worldwide. In 2014, sales were worth more than £521 million.

Albany's products and technologies help make paper smoother, tissue softer and aeroplane engines lighter through its two core businesses, Machine Clothing and Albany Engineered Composites. Albany International is the world's leading producer of custom-designed fabrics and belts essential to production in the paper, non-wovens and other process industries. Albany Engineered Components is a rapidly growing supplier of highly engineered composite parts for the aerospace industry.

Albany purchased James Kenyon and Son in 1968. Upon the closure of Derby Street Mills, it moved to its present site at Pilsworth which was a purpose-built mill for papermaking felts.

The site has undergone a number of improvements including two recent extensions to the building which were completed in 2008.

They effectively doubled the production area and allowed the company to produce a more diverse product range, further securing the company's position in the market and the role of the Bury site which produced dryer fabrics and press fabrics before its attention turned to its current product range. Among its output in the recent past has been cloth for the tennis balls used at Wimbledon.

Above: *Pilsworth site in 2013.* ***Top:*** *Installation of the weaving looms at the Pilsworth Mill in the early 70s.*

Currently, Albany produces process belts which are essential to the paper production process.

All Albany's products are incorporated into paper machines and most are exported. The site currently employs around 90 employees, more than a fifth of whom have worked for the company for 20 years or more – the longest serving for over 40.

The products manufactured in Bury are constantly under development and innovation keeps it competitive in a volatile industry. The team at Bury is always ready to meet the next challenge.

Above: *A shoe press belt.*

Jetchem Systems

Family firm's success story

It's an important year in the history of Jetchem Systems which is celebrating its 25th year in business.

Established in 1991 by directors Paul Taylor, Mark Taylor and Alan Bennie in the picturesque valley of Rossendale in Lancashire, Jetchem started as a small, family-run business employing four people.

The company produced stone and brick cleaning chemicals and specialised in high pressure water jetting units including trolley, trailer, van, and lorry mounted options, all built on site in the UK. The machines were sold and hired to contractors dealing with drain and sewer cleaning, concreting cutting, stone cleaning and descaling billets, having customers such as British Steel and British Rail.

Above: *Training personnel on the use of Jetchem units soon after the company was established.* ***Below:*** *Paul Taylor and Simon Nicholls at a trade show in Torbay they attended in 2000.*

As the company expanded, Allen Bennie resigned due to other commitments but remained firm friends. Andrew Taylor and Roland Taylor joined the board making the company a true family business.

The company expanded by purchasing Superjet, a water jetting manufacturer based in South Wales in 1999 and over the following years opened four more depots across the UK trading under the name of Superjet. Today, the company employs over 80 staff across six depots which have been strategically placed nationwide.

The company has always strived to offer a professional service while maintaining the values of a family-run business. It fast became one of the largest manufacturers of high and ultra high pressure water jetting equipment and accessories in the UK. It is now regarded as the one stop shop for water jetting equipment. The company covers practically every aspect of the industry, from training for water jetting, confined spaces, first aid and health and safety, to producing bespoke built units for both sale and hire to a very specialised market.

The company is always at the forefront of new technologies and methods including lining equipment, patch kits, resins, packers and lateral cutters for re-opening the lateral pipes after relining, which negates the need for excavation.

The firm not only supplies services covering the UK but also internationally, having manufactured and delivered to places such as Australia, Europe and the Middle East.

Jetchem still caters for small independent drainage contractors but is also able to meet the needs of councils and utility companies. A true success story for a local family-run business.

Left: *A recent photograph of the Jetchem head office team with some of the units.*

Hargreaves Ductwork Ltd

The industry of the tinker lives on

Hargreaves was founded in 1872 by Henry Hargreaves, a time-served tinsmith or 'tinker', in the Heywood/Cook Street area of Bury when he and his father began making baking tins and lawnmower boxes.

By the mid-1890s the company had acquired retail premises in Silver Street from where they traded as general ironmongers and bicycle assemblers. It was in this decade that the business began manufacturing ornate turret roof ventilators in tin and copper. Many of these were used on churches, schools, factories and theatres throughout the area.

In the 1950s the company began the manufacture of ductwork for heating, ventilation and air conditioning. Hargreaves began winning major contracts, first at the Shell Building in London, then during the manufacture of Concorde, where ductwork was used to blast hot and cold air on the machine to simulate the extreme conditions of supersonic flight.

In 1957 Hargreaves became Senior Hargreaves, following a takeover by Senior Group plc. The firm continued its growth by working on some of the UK's most notable buildings including The Barbican Centre, Tower Bridge, London City Hall, Portcullis House, Wembley and the Lloyd's Building, where Hargreaves' ductwork was used as a design feature.

In 2012 Hargreaves was acquired by MW High Tech Projects UK, retaining its revered trading name 'Hargreaves.' The company then began its new journey of development and growth in the specialist field of high integrity ventilation solutions as part of M-W in the UK, expanding into new markets and investing in new technology.

Above: The Cook Street factory in 1950. ***Top:*** A highly skilled welder at work.

Growth over the last 10 years has seen the strengthening of Hargreaves' retail outlets, the nationwide 'Trade Counters' which have bases from Hounslow to Aberdeen. With the development of these business facets, combined with the nationally recognised apprenticeship programme, Hargreaves remains one of the largest private sector employers in Bury.

To this day the ethos within Hargreaves remains one of customer focus, innovation and unparalleled quality, ensuring that the industry of the 'tinker' lives on in Bury through the continued manufacture of specialist ventilation and containment solutions.

HAMER & Co
BURY.
LHG559

ANGOULEME WAY

Left: As Bob Dylan sang in 1964, 'The Times They Are A Changin'. In this photograph from the same era, we can see the start of some of the vast changes to the shape, appearance and atmosphere, which took place over several decades in the centre of Bury. The old shopping area around Princess Street and Union Square was demolished in the late 1960s, and a concrete precinct emerged to replace it. This development was replaced by the Mill Gate Shopping Centre in the late 1990s. Cars parked on waste ground were to become a thing of the past, as Council planners, in most towns throughout the UK, attempted to improve traffic flow through the cluttered streets.

Below: On 6 October, 1971, the old Bury Market moved to the current site. The modern market hall pictured is like no other building featured in this book. It has modern glass and concrete styling with a bold 'gull-wing' roof, described as one of the best equipped and most architecturally striking market halls in the north-west. The final construction phase for Bury Market was completed in 1999 with the opening of the new purpose built 'Fish and Meat Hall' and the refurbishment of the outdoor market. Every year Bury Market attracts hundreds of thousands of shoppers drawn by the many bargains and sheer variety that can be found there. On regular market days, a visitor to the Fish and Meat Hall will be entertained by the theatre of the stallholders shouting out their wares and announcing the 'deals of the day'. In the present day the Market continues to provide a focal point for trade in Bury Town Centre and provides a stark contrast to the sterile environment of the modern day supermarket.

ACKNOWLEDGMENTS

The publisher would like to sincerely thank the following individuals and organisations for their help and contribution to this publication:

Bury Archives

PA Images

Barrie Kelly

All reasonable steps were taken by the publishers of this book to trace the copyright holders and obtain permissions to use the photographs contained herein. However, due to the passage of time certain individuals were untraceable. Should any interested party subsequently come to light, the publishers can be contacted at the phone number printed at the front of this book and the appropriate arrangements will then be made.